FAMILY LIFE AND THE CHURCH

Family Life and the Church

David M. Thomas

PAULIST PRESS
New York/Ramsey/Toronto

Library of Congress
Catalog Card Number: 79-90004

ISBN: 0-8091-2255-3

Published by Paulist Press
Editorial Office: 1865 Broadway, New York, N. Y. 10023
Business Office: 545 Island Road, Ramsey, N. J. 07446

Printed and bound in the
United States of America

CONTENTS

Chapter One

OPPORTUNITIES

Each of us, it is said, has his or her moment on the stage. What we do with our moment is left to our own ingenuity and sense of responsibility. There once was a Pope whose name was John Paul the First. His moment on the stage was quite brief, and some might call his role only that of a bit player, a cameo of sorts. But in his own unique way, in the person that he was and in the crucial moment he appeared, it seems that he significantly shifted the tone of the action. He presented to his audience of the world a smile that rose from the depths of his heart. And he was chosen by his brother prelates because he had a certain touch, a *feeling* for the people. He was chosen because he was above all else a *pastoral* man. While he was on stage, his lines although few were quite significant.

This book is about family life and how the Church might more effectively assist families to reach their full Christian potential. On September 21, 1978, John Paul I addressed a group of bishops from the United States in what became one of his few public speeches. The topic that he discussed was family life. His selection of a topic, he mentioned, was based on a desire to deal with an area of life that deeply touched the life of the Church. Here is some of what he said:

> **The Christian family is so important, and its role so basic in transforming the world and in building up the kingdom of God, that the Council called it a "domestic church" (*Lumen Gentium*, 11). Let us never grow tired of proclaiming the family as a community of love: conjugal love unites the couple and is procreative of new life. It mirrors divine love, is communicated and, in the words of "Gaudium et Spes" [Pastoral Constitution on the Church in the Modern World], is actually a sharing in the covenant of love of Christ and his Church (paragraph 48).[1]**

The life of the Christian family *is* part of the life of the Church. The very *life* of the family, particularly the quality of the relationships within the family, are the living cells of the Body of Christ which is the Church. What the Council saw, what John Paul I recalled, and what now stands as a central priority in the life of the Catholic Church in the United States, is all the same vision. It is a vision of the Christian family reaching for full Christian and human enrichment. This vision is one that focuses on the *basics* of life. It asks us to examine those experiences that are at the heart of life. It prompts us to reflect on those interpersonal relationships that constitute our personal Christian life. It forces us to be concrete in our thinking. It recalls that the love of the neighbor, which is at the center of a vital Christian life, is the love of one who lives next to you. For many this will mean a love that is a love

[1]Pope John Paul I, "On the Family," U.S.C.C. translation, 1978.

of family, a love of a marriage partner, a love of children, a love of parents.

Because the family is so fundamental in human life, any attempt to renew society or the Church will have to take into account the family reality. John Paul I knew this. He too was a man in touch with the human situation. With clarity and force, he stated:

The holiness of the Christian family is indeed a most apt means for producing the serene renewal of the Church which the Council so eagerly desired. Through family prayer, the "ecclesia domestica" [the domestic Church] becomes an effective reality and leads to the transformation of the world.[2]

When the Church speaks of renewal and transformation, it is important to sense the specific area of life that this concern touches. The Church is not concerned with material prosperity, with technological and scientific developments as basic elements of human change. What the Church presently judges to be crucial is the quality of how we relate to one another, our life of community. And so much of all that is community in our life is community in the family.

With a deep sense of urgency, John Paul I concluded his address to the bishops of the United States with these words:

Dear brothers, we want you to know where our priorities lie. Let us do everything we can for the Christian family, so that our people may fulfill their great vocation in Christian joy and share intimately and effectively in the Church's mission—Christ's mission—of salvation.[3]

The die has been cast. In a sense the Church is now in the process of collecting itself, its spirit and its resources in a wide-

[2] *Ibid.*
[3] *Ibid.*

spread effort, built on Christian hope, to renew itself through the renewal of Christian family life.

In May of 1978 the bishops of the United States unanimously approved the enactment of a comprehensive pastoral strategy to renew the life of the Christian family. Its efforts are summarized in what is called "The Plan of Pastoral Action for Family Ministry" (see Chapter Four). Pope John Paul II designated family life to be the topic of the international synod of the Roman Catholic Church in 1980. There is a spirit now manifest in the Church, a spirit of *these* times, and its concern is the family. This spirit calls into question all that the Church is doing to bring the Lord more fully into the life of the world. It is an invitation to assessment. If the Church is to do *everything* it can for the Christian family, as was the explicit wish of John Paul I and the apparent desire of the leadership of the Church in its many expressions, then it seems fitting to ask whether the Church can continue simply with what has been its pastoral methods of the past. Or is there a call for change? And if there is, to whom is that call addressed? Is it simply to the leadership, the bishops, the priests, the religious, the recognized lay leaders of the Church? Or is every member of the Church now under the power of the word to examine anew the relation of family life to Christian life? Is there something startling and immense happening in the Church the eventual resolution of which will significantly alter the landscape of the Church for years, perhaps centuries to come.

This is worth thinking about because there seems to be something alive in the Church causing some rather basic shifts in pastoral thinking and practices. It may be not only family life that is involved. In fact, there are probably significant alterations going on which will affect almost everything in Church life. It has been said that the reforms called for in the Council of Trent in the fifteenth century took about one hundred years to settle into the life of the Church in its many local settings. It has been a little more than a decade since the close of Vatican II. Perhaps the first real effects of the Council are now being felt. It's an exciting time to be alive as it happens!

If there were to be one word, one focal idea, one central image that would capture the spirit of the Church today, I would opt for the word *life*. Of course, a heightened sense of life is not simply the motif of Church life. In secular society what captures the attention of many is the pursuit of the good life, the peaceful life, the abundant life, the secure life, the life free from threat either environmental or social. It might be argued that in singling out life as a central image, we fall into the pit of generalization. Of course, life is what it's all about—that's obvious. But is it?

It is, *if* the quality of life is all that it should be. Given our particular concern for the life of families, we would have to ask the question: is the life of families healthy? In a Christian context we would add: do Christians appreciate and experience a richness of Christian life in the everyday experiences of their family life?

There are many ways to answer these questions and none of them are totally satisfactory. We could cite statistics on the number of broken marriages and abused children and parents, but the full story of the deep human experiences of acceptance, affirmation and caring is not easily translated into statistical patterns. Yet it is those very expressions that form the substance of healthy family life. Our statistics, although valid in themselves, often point to the last stages of family illness. What we need to focus on are the moments when our very humanity is created in the delicate, yet vital, interchanges of *ordinary* family life. It is the *spirit* of the family that is at issue. It is this spirit that concerns Christians and their Church as the effort is heightened to strengthen family spirit.

When discussing family life today, the word "crisis" often enters the conversation. Unfortunately we often view a crisis in the light of possible negative results. Crisis is a word that is used just before defeat or destruction. Perhaps we make this move toward a negative resolution because our media have exposed us for a long time to a rather consistent package of bad news. It is said to be more interesting to the viewer. So when we are told of a crisis, our ordinary reaction is to think that it will not be long before the really bad news is told.

There is, however, another meaning of crisis that dates back to an earlier usage when crisis meant both the possibility of good or bad. More than anything else, it meant that there was a shift in a situation, and that whatever would follow would be decisive. It meant opportunity, as the wheels of change were now turning.

So when we speak of a crisis in the Church, or a crisis in family life, we need not necessarily look for the white flag of surrender. Instead, we can take a careful account of where we now stand; we can honestly evaluate our resources at hand, and then plan a strategy that will make the best use of what we have. It sounds simple and in theory it is. What complicates the situation is that we are dealing with persons, not things. But the human factor does not prejudice the outcome. It only makes the process of improvement more of a challenge. It also means that our own human spirits will be taxed more fully.

Years ago, in the euphoria that accompanied the successful moon landings by the United States, television commentators liked to ask the question: if we can land a person on the moon, why can't we solve the problems of the cities, the schools, poverty and so forth. Sometimes they discussed urban poverty as if it were the same *kind* of problem as that of moving a certain payload of material, human or otherwise, to a distant spot in outer space. Of course they were quite wrong. One was simply a problem of physics and technology. The other was a problem of flesh and bone, of freedom and feeling, of prejudice and history. The two issues are light years apart in terms of difficulty. No one doubts this anymore.

There is a lesson in all this that cannot be overlooked when we are talking about family life or renewal in the Church. What we are dealing with is utterly human and it touches on what is most human in us, our relationships with one another.

So we should be careful not to accept a short-cut method of correction or improvement. And if we decide to enter the movement for family life (and through it, for the renewal of the Church), we should also be prepared for a rather long and demanding journey. Most of all, we will be forewarned by the advice of

Pogo—that in meeting the "enemy" we encounter ourselves! It's one thing to plot the improvement of another. It's a bit more sticky frankly to contemplate self-improvement.

We have now introduced two foundational concepts into the discussion: life and crisis. Taken together, it is interesting to note that they form the cognate word "life-crisis" that is of significant interest today. The topic of life-crisis usually arises in a description of the developmental phases of human life. Recently, there has been a whole library of books on this topic, particularly with reference to the stages of adult life. It appears that we are not finished with resolving growing pains with the completion of adolescence. It may even be that the trials of puberty are small compared with the challenges of adulthood, particularly the ominous ordeal of the so-called mid-life crisis.

What we might note about the discussion of life-crisis is its commonness and normality. It serves as a reminder that human life involves some hard edges, some rough spots; in the words of Erma Bombeck, we find that when promised cherries, we often end up with only the pits. We might ask ourselves the basic question: is this what it's all about? In the context of our concern for family life might we expect to encounter there not so much "home sweet home" as a real testing-ground for the true caliber of our humanity? For many the second option will ring most true.

In the United States particularly, we have ever to be on guard not to be fooled, and therefore hurt, by the various myths that surround family life and marriage. Most of them include the ideas that the home is sacred, the family is somehow an exception to the ordinary challenges of interpersonal life and that marriage is some automatic state of bliss if love exists. Far from being an exception to the dynamics of interpersonal life, family life usually brings out what's best and worst in us. It is a real testing of the authenticity of our love for others. It is a hothouse of what communal life is.

Any program designed to improve the quality of family life will have to be both *realistic* and *imaginative*. The need for realism is based quite simply on the fact that within the family so much of the real world comes to life. We touch others and they in turn touch us. Our fundamental sense of whether we are valued in ourselves, beyond the contributions we may make to the society at large, is conditioned by the experience of acceptance from those with whom we live. Likewise, our acceptance of others is tested by our willingness to accept those we *really* know. Most often, these will be the members of our own family.

Occasionally, we may hear some argue that love and concern for one's own family can be detrimental to the good of society in general. They will argue that love of one's family can be a love that is turned inward and that it is therefore not wholesome. These criticisms deserve to be heard because it can happen that our concern for family life will be such that it is used as an excuse for not meeting responsibilities outside the family. Our family can be an escape we use to flee from a concern for others, particularly if they are different from us. We argue that one has to take care of those at home first. Charity begins (and ends) there!

We will discuss this at length later (see Chapter Seven). Here we would note, however, that one can also become quite eloquent over meeting the needs of the hungry and homeless in distant lands, while neglecting the needs of those with whom one lives. Obviously, it is a question of a balance founded on a sincere and honest appraisal of one's resources, including such intangible resources as one's time and attention, as one attempts to live an authentic life of Christian love. This need for appraisal is present all the time. The price of a truly responsible life is a willingness to ask honest questions of oneself. Also to be noted is that this topic should be one regularly aired within the family. That can be a special way in which individual family members challenge one another to ever greater generosity.

Programs for family life renewal should be marked by the qualities of realism and imagination. There is a very practical reason for this and it is based on the principles of marketing. To sell a new product, you have first to capture the buyer's attention. The problem of program implementation today is made difficult by the fact that many people complain that there are not enough hours in the day as it is. They simply do not have enough time for additional activities or responsibilities. These complaints must be heard. They are real and in a way express one of the fundamental problems of family life. Individual family members have so many obligations right now that they do not have time for each other! We all need occasionally to stop and reflect on the pace of our lives and whether we are using our time, a most precious resource to be sure, in the best possible way. The question here is one concerning the time we spend with each other. It is also a question about what takes place in that time passed together. This is a most difficult point to examine because there exists no clear set of criteria against which one might make a reasonable assessment. One point can be made, however, which is that physical togetherness is not enough. Some meaningful, supportive conversation ought to be occurring within the family. And it ought to take place in longer segments than during the commercial breaks of the evening menu of television offerings.

A major intent of the Church in renewing family life is not to create widespread guilt feelings on the part of marriage partners and parents. The Lord knows that our efforts to live a loving communal life will often result in feelings of frustration and occasionally conclude in outright failure. Even in those moments, however, he is with us inviting us to begin again with renewed vigor and hopefulness.

Furthermore, the Church is not expecting families to add to their already filled schedule of activities. There is no plan to increase the heavy burden of responsibilities now sensed. Rather the intent is to awaken in families the resources of life and love that are *already* there. The Church is moving toward what might be called *Christian family empowerment*. In a sense, the Church is saying that it wants no more of families than the full flowering of the latent Christian potential they already possess.

An imaginative way of describing this latent potential of families is necessary because of the long-standing separation of Church or religious life from the very ordinary events of daily life. It is all too common for us to equate religious activity with what goes on in the church building and to forget that the untold expressions of recognition, acceptance and forgiveness that go on in the home are the kernel of one's authentic religious life. In other words, more genuine Christian activity may go on in the backyard than in the back pew. This is not to argue for an either/or situation, but to expand our awareness of the real possibility of a both/and context for real Christianity. If Christianity is alive in our day, it will be found in those areas of human life where we are most involved. It will be a part of both the cheers and the cries of life. It will be at those soft and hard edges where we touch one another. The Lord pointed us in the right direction when he described authentic religion as a matter of the heart. The heart was thought to be the center of one's life. It was the originating point from which all the decisive activities of the person came. If the heart was going in the right direction, one's total life would be rightly focused.

In calling special attention to family life, the Church is simply reading the situation of contemporary Christianity in the light of that overused phrase "where people are at." It is saying that where vital relational life unfolds, the vitality of the Christian life must also be present. It is also saying that the life of a "Church person" must involve more than being counted on the rolls of a directory of dues-paying members. To be in the genuine Church community of the Lord means that one is alive *communally* to the workings of the Spirit in the everyday events of this extraordinary life we have all been given. It means that we are open to the people with whom we live. We are responsive to their needs and feelings as we allow ourselves to be exposed to them. It is to live out in practice the interrelation of the love of God and the love of neighbor. It is to know the reason why the Lord said that the grand examination at the end of our life would be one when many questions would be asked concerning our personal responsiveness to the *interpersonal* events of our many days. Given the fact that so many of these events are, in some manner, family events, it would also have to be said with boldness and clarity in the Church which is invited to make present the wishes of its Lord, that the Lord is concerned about family life! This was clearly the message of Vatican II.

Two themes of Church life have been woven into the tapestry that we call the spirit of the contemporary Church. They are the call to mission and the invitation to communal life. The call to mission stresses that the Church is the concrete continuation of the work of Jesus through the centuries. This work is based on a deep appreciation of the incredible love of God that stands behind the wondrous events of creation and redemption. It is the imperfect, yet authentic, attempt on the part of humanity to enflesh that concern of God in the lives of real people. The call to community also flows from our sense of being loved and accepted as the kind of people we really are. We are invited to be in touch with God. We are drawn into his friendship. We must also be genuinely turned toward our neighbor. These foundational insights will color the many areas where family life will concern the Christian.

It should now be clear that the Christian life and family life are to be integrated in a very thorough manner. The matter deserves careful reflection and discussion. In the words of *The Music Man*, we have to know the territory. Let us turn now to a discussion of some of the more significant features of family life today.

Chapter Two

THE HUMAN
CONTEXT OF
FAMILY LIFE

ARTISTIC PORTRAYALS OF JESUS in the Renaissance give the impression that he was an Italian who lived in the hills outside of Florence. Not only did he have the appearance of a Florentine, but he was garbed in the finery of the day and was often depicted in the marketplace of that bustling city. Historical purists might complain over the artistic freedom taken by the painters. But the artists would respond with an interesting and rather genuine *theological* argument: Jesus was the *incarnate* Word of God who truly lived on this earth. Unless you consider him simply a historical figure who lives only in memory—which would be a most unchristian interpretation—then you should picture him in some way in touch with the real world of each historical period. Talented with brush and oil, the Renaissance artists did just that. They placed Jesus at the corner of Tuscany Boulevard and Mediterranean Drive! Unmistakably he was present in their world.

This same sense comes through in reading the New Testament. Jesus was a first-century Galilean who deeply identified with the hopes and fears of his contemporaries (as he does now too). He spoke their language and allowed them to feel fully at home and accepted in his presence. He was not aloof or distant. He was almost too close to them in that many expected a grandiose Messiah, and he did not fill that picture. He wanted to show that God was with his people in all the vicissitudes of their ordinary life. He came to transform their real lives, not something imaginary existing in some pipe dream.

When he finally departed in visible form, he left his followers with a warning. In the story of his Ascension the disciples are described as gazing toward the clouds, rapt in attention for the figure who had just left their presence. The warning was that they should not look up there, but toward each other and toward the world and get busy spreading the message and the life which Jesus stood for. They were to be in touch with each other and with the events of this earth because the Lord had not really left. He was truly still present as was discovered by some on the way to Emmaus and by another on the way to Damascus.

The same must be said about Christianity today. It will always be "tainted" by the world. It must be if it is to exercise the transforming power of the Spirit. It is both the duty and the privilege granted Christians to be concerned about this life and to be terribly involved in its happenings.

The world is always changing and according to most who describe these changes, it is changing at a rate unprecedented in human history. This means that the Church more than ever must be in touch with this human reality to formulate its theology and design its programs so that they really describe the incarnated reality of the Christian life. This is not to say that the Church mimics or merely repeats whatever is fashionable at a given time. There must be a critical interplay of the demanding Word of God and the need of the human reality which results in the Christian meaning coming through the human situation. The point here is simply that the Church must be aware of that which it is commissioned to proclaim: the continued *incarnated* presence of the Spirit of God in the flesh-and-bone lives of real persons.

What is the human reality that concerns us here? It is family life. We must ask then: what is the shape of family life today? What kind of pressures are families beset with? Are these good times or bad times for families?

Certainly one can get the ear of most people more quickly by reciting some doomsday statistics. For some reason we moderns have a penchant for apocalyptic warnings that the last days are upon us. You would think that we would be more interested in good news and accounts of all the good things that are happening today. A case in point would be the typical recitation of statistics on divorce. Often one reads that one-third of all marriages end in divorce. (I do not want to get into the debate over the meaning or interpretation of this right here.) My question is: why not begin with the statistic that two-thirds of all marriages will not end in divorce, and add that many of the divorced will remarry and have better marriages than their former ones?

One should also mention that the worthwhile meaning of statistics lies in their interpretation. And it must be remembered that numbers are really persons and that beneath each number is a human story of both pain and joy. This most certainly has to be remembered in the area of family life where so much of our deeply personal life is experienced.

Statistics can of course tell us something significant. For instance, the family situation is now quite *varied*. While a common stereotype of the average family may assume that the two-parent, two-child family is typical, statistically that combination ends up being only 6.8 percent of the family scene. Another common portrait of the family in which the father is gainfully employed and the mother is at home with the children who are growing up also turns out to be, in fact, a rarity. That pattern is present only in 16 percent of the families of the United States. In 1978 more than one-half the mothers of America were employed outside the home. And each year the percentage of single parents rises significantly. So when one attempts to imagine the typical family, one has to bring forth a number of scenarios. Also, one has to be open to even further modifications as the family scene continues to adapt to the particular dynamics of life today. It should also be added that these variations of family composition cut across religious lines. The Catholic family of the last quarter of the twentieth century, at least structurally, is practically a carbon copy of its non-Catholic neighbors.

If we take a broad enough sweep across recent history, some rather basic shifts in the context of family life can be described. In the United States, we can begin with a description of the rather self-sufficient family farm with the family as the basic social unit providing practically every human need. Following this often romanticized setting, the dominant pattern of family life shifts to the city as the industrial revolution takes hold of American life. The center of life expands to the neighborhood, the factory and the local parish church. The purely functional role of the family in bringing up children and providing for the economic well-being of the family members is shared with other societal units. There remains, however, a rather set pattern of survival and relating. Mobility, either social or geographical, is limited. The primary societal influences remain the family, the local community and what is generally referred to as "tradition."

In most recent times the shift has been away from the cities to the suburbs as the industrial revolution gives way to the age of technology. Of course, technology has been with humanity since our early ancestors figured out that you could get more done with a sharpened rock than with a closed fist. But the impact of modern technology is now so pervasive that much of what we term the unique condition of contemporary family life can be explained by inventions and techniques that were unknown in the time of our grandparents. Since these many innovations come to the family from the outside, it is understandable that the family might complain of being put upon by forces it is incapable of controlling.

In fact, it is this feeling of powerlessness over its own affairs that may be the dominant feeling of the family today. Parents often feel that their efforts to parent effectively are cancelled out by forces outside the family. Families feel that their attempts to plan for their own future are often wasted because of the many unexpected and undesired events that interrupt those plans. The problems created by today's economic situation is a case in point. With a spiraling inflation rate, with energy costs escalating each year, with the increased costs of basic items (food, shelter and clothing), is it any surprise that families experience stress touching almost every corner of their lives? The words of a Paul Simon song ring true: "My life is made of patterns that can scarcely be controlled."

It seems that it is only with great difficulty that a hopeful description for families can be drawn. Nevertheless, it must be attempted to avoid submitting to what is perhaps the most destructive tendency of all, namely, that of despair. The reason that despair is unchristian is that it is the game plan of the quitter, the dropout and the fatalist. The attitude of despair implies that we are abandoned exclusively to our own totally limited resources. Or it holds that we are under the power of an alien force that is not supportive of our best future. It cannot be stated too strongly that despair is opposed to everything that Christianity stands for. That is why it is so incumbent upon the Christian to see *in* the human situation zones of hopefulness where a full investment of effort and energy can be directed. It was in this spirit that Vatican II continually called for a reading of the spirit of the times. This was not simply to insure the relevance of Christianity, but to hold that *within* the human situation were the God-given ingredients that would be the building-blocks of the Kingdom of God in each historical period. It is also to say that the raw material is *always* available. The problem for Christianity has ever been to find laborers willing to mine that raw material.

Any description of the human horizon will bear of course the imprint of the one who creates the picture. No apologies are necessary for this because none of us can step outside his or her skin and assume a nonsubjective posture. All that each of us can do is to cross check our observations with those of others in the hope that eventually major areas of agreement will result.

Admittedly, then, the following description is somewhat contrived. What I will do is first to present five conditions in contemporary America which provide a milieu of hope for families as they seek both simple survival and increased vitality. This is presented first in compliance with the contention that hopefulness is a fundamental disposition of the Christian in the world. I quite knowingly did not say optimism because there is a certain determinism in the attitude of optimism that can stand in the way of a full and responsive human effort. The Christian life is an invitation to activity. It is a charge to be a kingdom-builder. Success in that venture really depends on the generosity of the human spirit. It also depends on the availability of the Lord's guidance and assistance, but that has already been promised! What is needed is us. That was the risk that God took in creating us with the gift of freedom. Hopefulness rests on the belief that God is with us, behind us and ahead of us. But *we* must move as we are moved by God. Please do not, however, expect a totally clear picture of this process of collaboration. It is not necessary because the process is much easier to live out than it is to explain.

After presenting these five areas of hope, I will offer five areas of contemporary life that work to deplete the vitality of family life. These give cause for realistic concern and a context for meaningful resistance when they prove to disintegrate family life.

Beginning on our note of hope, I see five aspects of contemporary life which enhance the possibility of a positive resolution to the everyday demands of family living. They are: (1) the possession of better knowledge of the human person and the dynamics of interpersonal living; (2) a greater range of possibilities in dealing with difficult situations; (3) a greater capability of free association with others who can assist us in overcoming problems;

(4) better health and (5) the availability of religious support that is geared to sustaining a vital relational life.

The first point is based on the view that we are the beneficiaries and the victims of what is often called "the knowledge explosion." We often forget that the human sciences of psychology, anthropology and sociology are youngsters in the academy of sciences. Nevertheless, our understanding of the human situation has been enhanced immensely by the insights of these inquiries. We have learned for instance that in many ways we must respect our humanity with its complex rhythms and harmonies. We have learned that the acquisition of interpersonal intimacy takes time and effort. We have learned that each of us has basic needs that must be respected or else we harm ourselves and do harm to the relationships which are most dear to us. We have learned about the many sides of communication: the role of silent language, the value of honest exchange and the need for quiet so that our thoughts may be gathered, examined and fashioned in communicable form. We have realized that acts of apparent hostility are often masked cries for help or acknowledgment. We have learned of the many emotional needs of children as they begin their journey into the world of complex adulthood. We have learned that even adult life carries with it particular crises that help explain some of the tensions we all feel at certain moments of adulthood.

In all this we are able to be more realistic about what we might expect of ourselves and others. We can more easily adjust to unexpected experiences, knowing that they are simply part of the ordinary fare of human existence. We are less vulnerable to coming under the power of destructive myths about life in general, about communal life and the experiences of intimacy. We are less likely to seek resolutions in the stars or in some magic formula that promises to quiet our fears or erase our problems in an instant without any expenditure of the human spirit.

A second benefit of life today is our ability to consider effectively alternative ways of solving inevitable human problems. In other words, we have more freedom to act. In the language of history and sociology, in earlier times there were rather fixed social systems. One's birth cemented one into a particular lifestyle and significantly determined where one lived, what one did as an occupation and, in many cases, even determined whom one would marry. What was more inhibiting, however, was the lack of possible alternatives in thought or modes of behavior. Today we have what is called a pluralistic situation. Our society tolerates an incredible variety of lifestyles and living patterns. Of course, some will argue that there are liabilities in the present scheme. Under the older system both certainty and security were more possible. One knew where one fit and what was expected in particular situations. Marriage patterns and parenting styles were rather uniform.

We have rather scant information about the quality of family life in those more structured times. What literature we have seems to indicate that most relational energy was expended outside the marital and family framework. Therefore, one of the apparent benefits of our new social order is the opening up of marital and family life to new intensities of relational living. In that sense, then, those who praise the "good old days" may have a rather fanciful sense of what really took place in families, and their nostalgia may tell us more about them than it does about history!

The new pluralism and toleration in allowing us more freedom of choice gives us, of course, greater latitude to enrich or to destroy ourselves. Given the broad propensities of human nature, we can expect to see, on the one hand, wonderful families and marital unions. We can also on the other hand expect to tell the story of human tragedies in marriage and family life.

A third benefit supporting family life today is the greater freedom we have to associate with others. We can make better choices of marital partners and can select friends who are truly supportive. With the benefits of modern communication, we can keep in touch although we are separated by distance. The jammed telephone lines on major holidays give evidence to untold family reunions taking place.

With the change to a basically technological culture, less time and work are necessary to keep society operating at full productivity. The average work-week has been lessening consistently since the beginning of this century. This means that there is at least the opportunity for the family to be together for greater periods of time. I said "opportunity." Many families will complain that they *never* get together. Here would be a case where a *positive* use of freedom could work wonders.

Each family will work out its own style of associations. Obviously, a healthy balance of life inside and outside the family is desirable. The point is not to argue that this balance regularly takes place. Here we seek only a clarification of the creative possibilities available to families should they have the desire and the spirit to take advantage of them.

Association with the helping professions is also a more common experience today. It is rare today that one would be stigmatized for consulting a psychiatrist. In some social circles it may even be considered normal. Also, the growing practice of family therapy provides much needed help for families who have painted themselves into an emotional corner and need a trained outsider to point them in a direction away from whatever destructive patterns may be operating.

Under freedom of association I would also mention the various methods now available for marriage partners to assist them in improving their own relationship. While Marriage Encounter is the most well known, there are springing up around the country many promising programs for marriage and family enrichment. We are at a point in history when there is an incredible felt need for authentic intimacy and sincere friendship *in* marriage and family life. And there seems no slacking off in this interest. This is indeed a sign of hope!

A fourth benefit for family life today is quite simply the possibility of better health. We may overlook this benefit although we should not because the health-care revolution is one of the distinguishing high points of this century. To appreciate this benefit fully one would have to recall the all-too-common situation of just a few decades ago when maternal- and infant-mortality rates were quite high. Debilitating diseases were known in almost every family. Sickness was simply a fact of life that had to be endured. Penicillin and other modern drugs were unknown. We now live longer lives, which means the opportunity for the development of deeper relationships. Again, it is a case of the opportunity being there; people can't be forced to use it creatively or beneficially.

One should also include advances in the treatment of mental disorders. It goes without saying that fundamental distortions of one's ability to perceive reality or to relate freely and openly with others erodes family life significantly. But with a greater understanding of the causes and treatment of mental disorders, light appears at the end of a tunnel where, at one time, there was only darkness. Beneficial also is the actual use of one's family in the therapeutic process.

And lastly, although by no means the least important, is the development of theological descriptions in Christianity, and in other major religions as well, that stress the importance of interpersonal relations in authentic religion. There is a growing consensus among Christians that being a follower of the Lord necessarily includes the pursuit of a life shared with others. Intimacy with God will ordinarily include intimacy with others. In some cases, the experience of God will come primarily through one's life with others. This is not the place to elaborate the point. It will form the substance of the next chapter where we will discuss the theology of marriage and family life. Here we would stress only that the full motivational energy of a person religiously alive can be brought to bear on the many interpersonal experiences of life. For many of us, that will primarily be the relationships within our families.

Five facets of contemporary life have been offered to support the position that there are genuine signs of hope for the future of Christian family life. These conditions, and many others that each of us will be able to speak about if we are on the lookout for their presence, are truly fortuitous. But there exist other factors in modern life that function in an opposite way. They serve to pull us apart. Their power is to preclude community. Knowledge of their nature and extent is a first step in overcoming their injurious influence.

The five tendencies that operate in a way adverse to healthy family life are: (1) the exaggerated importance accorded material possessions; (2) the pervasive cult of self-fulfillment; (3) the short-range approach to commitment and friendship; (4) the ready availability of convenient escape routes from problem situations and (5) the influence of television.

Materialism is no newcomer as an issue in human life, but it has taken on some new dimensions in recent years that have a rather decisive influence on many families. Clearly we need material resources to survive. Such resources aid us in enjoying the good creation of God. Christianity is not an anti-materialistic religion. In fact, with its sacramental sensitivity, it invites us to relish the things of this earth as part of the way we grow in an understanding of God.

What should be noticed, however, is that material reality is not an end in itself, but a stepping stone to its origin in God. What we see so often in the modern world is the sense that material possessions are goals in themselves. We see people literally spending their lives trying to own the best and the most. Their willingness to embark on that journey is greatly supported by the general value structure of American life which is geared to the production and the *consumption* of more and more.

Part of the strategy of this value structure is to expand the list of potential buyers by stressing that every single person should possess as many things as possible. For families, particularly if they are large, this philosophy has ominous consequences. One television set will never do; each person needs his or her own room; to share a stereo smacks of communism; everyone needs his or her own set of wheels. One test of whether this philosophy has entered your own life is to ask yourself: how do you feel about borrowing, especially from neighbors? Years ago, the borrowed cup of sugar was a symbol of neighborly interdependence. Are such exchanges as common today? Are we uncomfortable in asking for favors? Do we apologize before we ask a neighbor whether we can borrow a garden tool or a few slices of bread? My contention is that we have learned well the lesson of the advertisers who are the preachers of American business: do not be beholden to anyone! If you are, you are weak, irresponsible and not a credit to our nation. In other words, our national goal is: private things for private people!

A second destructive influence on family life is what might be called the cult of self-fulfillment. It has many nuances that require much more discussion than can be given here. In many ways it is at the heart of the problem of practically every social issue facing contemporary America. Its roots can be traced back to the very origins of the United States. For instance, how many of us realize that there was *no* intention to create a *united* set of colonies after the issuance of the Declaration of Independence? Much of the rhetoric spilled during our recent celebration of the Bicentennial was in contrast to the intentions of the original drafters of the document of 1776. They did not want to form a country of interdependent states. They wanted independence and freedom not only from the mother country, but also from each other!

The story of life today in America continues to be a tension between independence and interdependence. This conflict cuts across the political scene, the economic world, the educational debates and even enters the sacred precincts of the home. It most tellingly affects the life of the family!

The philosophy of self-fulfillment tells us first of all to follow our personal inclinations no matter what. It calls us to be self-sufficient. It tells us to stand on our personal ground and defend it courageously. It's a philosophy based on the principle of competition that sees victory only in winning. It does not value cooperation, sharing, mutuality, or community. It cannot understand personal sacrifice unless the act of sacrifice results in heroic acclaim for the person who does the good deed. It accepts the principle that it is in giving that we receive, as long as we receive a lot in the giving. In other words, it twists altruistic virtue into its own framework of self-centeredness.

My description is rather one-sided and it may not apply literally to any particular person. But the influence of this anti-relational worldview is alive and well in contemporary America. In family life it sets itself into the decision-making process as a ''me-first" argument in some, or even all, judgments affecting that intimate community. At best this method of solving problems results in compromise; at worst, it ends up simply being the survival of the fittest—or the loudest. Commonly what happens is that the individual family members simply settle into a routine of living their own lives and come together only when it is convenient and in the best interests of each member taken individually. A symptom of this process of separation or withdrawal is the increased sound of silence among family members. They seem to have less and less in common. What conversation takes place is usually superficial and routine. For practical purposes each person lives a private life, neither touching nor being touched by those whom they see every day, and who merely share the same address.

How did such a state of affairs come to be? Most probably it was a gradual development. It stems, however, quite logically from the philosophy of individualism that sees perfection as "atomized" development. In taking care of myself, I will find satisfaction. In building my own empire, I will gain fulfillment. There are many variations on this theme, but it seems always to come down to a fundamental unwillingness to move out of the world of self-interest and include in one's life, in a meaningful way, the lives of others. This move to others is, of course, the basis of a Christian worldview—which is also to say that some who *call* themselves Christians are not because they don't necessarily subscribe to an other-centered view of life.

It is important to add here that hasty judgments about particular persons or movements ought not to be made. For instance, to brand the women's liberation movement as self-centered would overlook the complexity of the issues involved and groundlessly project motives on people without adequate evidence. Likewise, there are moments in the lives of all of us when we must consider our own needs first, both out of a responsibility to ourselves and to be the best person we can for others. Like an undetected cancer that has been infecting one's body for many years, the malady of individualism may be widespread before a clear recognition of its presence is possible. What is needed, however, is a good sense of its "danger signs."

Poor communication between family members, persons pre-
ferring to be alone almost continually, meals taken in haste with
no regard for persons present or absent, leisure activities done
alone or with others but never with members of one's own family,
a breakdown in the common expressions of acknowledgment and
gratitude, an increase in the use of the common escapes in the
home, alcohol and television—these are all indications that the
cancer is present and spreading and something will have to
change unless "family" becomes only a nice word signifying
nothing!

A third erosive force is a lack of permanency in relationships.
There are many reasons for this in contemporary life. First, we are
a very mobile population. Many families are spread from coast to
coast. Friends are friends for only a while, then they or we pull up
tent stakes and move on to another site. Our interests change too.
We are "into" this or that only until we tire or our tools or
gadgets break. Then we look for something new to "get into."
And we feel of course that there is no reason to stay committed to
something whether it is a profession, or a neighborhood or a
religion or a family. To be modern is to be fluid, to hang loose.
We may say that we have the world by the tail, but if we look
closely, we may be holding only the tail!

We moderns value the immediate. We suck all the juice from
what we have in hand right now. We hear it said that you can't
count on the future: Get what you can right now. Symptomatic of
this spirit is the incredible turnover of our material goods. Maybe
they don't build things the way they used to, but we don't mind
because we don't want them that long anyway. We allow ourselves to be attracted to the latest fashions in clothing, furniture,
appliances, and gadgets because we have allowed ourselves to
believe that the latest or the newest has to be the best.

Of course we can resist this mood, but in doing so, we will
definitely feel out of step with the rest of society. We will also be
doing things that may not be understood by others. For instance,
we will find ourselves working on friendships, wasting time with
people; we will be taking risks by saying what's on our mind and
in our heart, especially with those with whom we live. We will

allow ourselves to feel the pain of loss or separation. We will invest in relationships as if they were to last a lifetime, while in the back of our mind we know that they probably will not. We may relocate geographically quite often, but we will carry our friends with us in our hearts and it will both feel good and hurt an awful lot. Such is the price of fidelity.

A fourth force affecting relationships is the easy-way-out approach to interpersonal stress. It can be divided into a technological and a sociological form. Under the former, we could list the ease of traveling away from our problems, especially by automobile. It might include escape into a world of sight and sound through television and the stereo, or simply escape into a private space either in the home or elsewhere. There is also the escape brought by drugs, especially on the well-known path lubricated by alcohol. There is escape into the world of one's job or one's hobbies or just into compulsive activity. This latter escape is generally rewarded by the compliment that you are really a "hard worker."

Also, there is the total escape from interpersonal strains which is simply to leave. About all that can be said about such a "solution" is that it is easier to leave today than it was yesterday. To have on your record that you are divorced is no great social stigma. This is not to belittle the pain of divorce for all those who are touched by it. But it is to say that divorce seems to be a realistic solution to marital problems for an increased number of persons in our society, regardless of religion or social position. There are also the many separations, desertions, abandonments and rejections that never enter the official rolls.

There are inevitable tensions and moments of conflict when people live together. The problem is not how to avoid conflict. It is rather how to resolve conflict for the best of all those involved and for the communal life that they share. More than ever, families need not only skills of relating that can overcome differences which create discord, but also the skills to move on to even stronger bonds of closeness after the dust from battle has settled. These might be termed "skills of reconciliation." In Chapter Six we will discuss relationships within the *Christian* family and this topic will be amplified.

A fifth factor in contemporary life that merits discussion because of its potentially destructive bent is the television set. Here we might have considered the total impact of the media: movies, books, magazines, radio—and find ample reason for concern over their combined effect on family vitality. We might become too generalized, however, and perhaps miss the fact that effects of television, in terms of quantitative impact, dwarf those of all other media. Television is part of almost everyone's daily life. It affects all ages, all social classes, all who have eyes to see and ears to hear. Again, we cannot hope to give an adequate description of television's effect on us. In reality, no one really knows this because its influence is so pervasive.

There are many ways of examining television's influence on family life. We could point to the dominant messages on the tube: its emphasis on high-powered action, its offering of quick solutions to complex human problems, its exaggerated portrayal of the everyday drama of life, its fostering of the myth of the quick win, its superficial and adolescent way of presenting human sexuality, and on and on. We should also mention the way it explicitly presents family life. The basic question here should be: is that portrayal realistic? Or is it designed simply to entertain, to shock or to poke fun at? How often is the "put-down" the common style of relating? To phrase the matter in a general question: does the *content* of contemporary American television contribute *anything* to the enrichment of family life?

Another aspect of television is the *time* it consumes in our lives. We are all familiar with the statistics in this matter. It's roughly three to four hours per day for each of us. Given the fact that a large segment of our time is taken by sleep, work, eating and travel, that doesn't leave much left for anything else, particularly if we take three or more hours off the top for the tube.

Some will no doubt respond that the family at least *gathers* around the set. It is their time together. They converse during the shows; they snack together during the commercials. Granted that such togetherness is probably better than none at all, the family ought to ask itself about the *quality* of their togetherness in the circumstances. This issue is further affected by the kind of human response ordinarily drawn forth by television viewing. Generally, it is a rather passive form of activity. The fact that so many people fall asleep before the fluttering screen suggests its soothing effect. Also you can do a lot of other things while watching the set and still be mildly involved.

Admittedly, then, you can do other things while watching television. But what is the quality of such interrelationships? A visitor who knew nothing about television but a lot about family life may be difficult to persuade that television viewing and family togetherness are a good mix.

Television can also be a ready escape from issues that should be faced. This is related to the many escapes available today and mentioned earlier. The question here is: what conversations should have taken place but didn't because the potential discussants were watching television instead? Do we turn on the set to forget our troubles? That is often a point brought up to explain the popularity and the *content* of daytime television.

What does a constant stream of television do to our minds? Educators are deeply concerned about this issue. Are the lower national test scores of today's students brought about by the type of thinking they have fallen into as they "adjusted" to the mindset of television? What about our ability to be logical, perceptive, creative?

What is apparent here is that many questions crop up when the impact of television is discussed. It clearly merits a special listing among those items in contemporary society that serve to undermine the vitality of the family.

We included this chapter to note the human influences that affect Christian family life. We must also stress the Christian vision of marriage and family, and to this most serious and exciting discussion we now turn.

Chapter Three

THE THEOLOGY OF MARRIAGE AND FAMILY LIFE

Out of the experience of Christians who are married and live in families, and from the inspired tradition of the Church comes a theology. This theology describes the life story of countless Christians through the centuries who have been in contact with the living Spirit, and who have expressed that reality in the everyday encounters of home and family. Some of that story worked its way into the writings of theologians, some of it became a part of the Church's liturgy, some of it was fashioned into the law of the Church. Like all the theology of the Church, it is open to development and renewal. It grows as it is lived out and discussed both in the intimate conversation of married Christians with their God and in the dialogue that takes place among concerned Christians. This theology is founded on faith and on the living relation of persons with God. It is a story both personal and communal. It lives in words and books. But more fundamentally it lives in the lives of married Christians.

What we propose here is a survey of recent insights into the Christian meaning of marriage and family life. As will become apparent, much of this discussion is dependent on the theological wisdom present and operative in the Church in Vatican II and its effect on the present. This period of the Church's life shows not only a rich development in the theological understanding of marriage and family life, but also a strenghtening of pastoral concern for married Christians and their families. In fact, what seems to be occurring in the Church is a tangible revolution with regard to the concern for and the support of marriage and family life. As this becomes more of a pastoral priority in the Church, we can expect our understanding of marriage and family life to deepen and grow more complete. In a way what follows ought to be viewed as the description of a beginning, a seeding of the imagination of the Church, an account of the Christian journey at this time, but not necessarily the exact tale that will be told farther down the road.

The most significant Christian feature of marriage and family life is that it is a special expression of one's life *in* the Church. Recent theological understanding of the Church has emphasized that it is above all else the life of a community. The Church is a community created from the life-giving water and blood that flowed from the pierced side of Jesus on the cross. It is a communal life nourished by the life-enriching bread of Christ's body given in celebration.

Christian family life is filled with moments of intimacy, acceptance, caring and support. From a human standpoint these expressions of interpersonal warmth are indispensable for the development of the human personality. From a Christian standpoint they are required so that the love of God may again take on human form and become a part of the personal history of each Christian. To put it simply: The Church *needs* the Christian family!

In theory we may be able to speak of the love of God, about the love that gives birth to the creation of the universe and to each person who is invited to live in God's garden. But it is also necessary to point to the enfleshed expressions of God's love. To do this Christians first tell each other the story of God's love in the life of Jesus. They tell about the care Jesus expressed for everyone he met. They tell about his kindness especially for those on the edge of society, those forgotten by the side of the road. They tell the startling story of God's love even for sinners, those who have smacked God's face and yet receive a welcome back into his waiting arms. They tell the story of how, after the Resurrection of Jesus, Christians continued to express God's love in imitation of Jesus. What is also clear in their story-telling is that it often mentions the love *among* the members of the Christian community. They note that Jesus himself said that *their love for each other* would be a distinguishing mark that God was truly present among them.

While it is seemingly easy to admit the need for authentic love in the Christian community, we should be aware that the reality must also be present. There is always a tendency to "intellectualize" or "romanticize" love in the Church. We spin fine theories about the various definitions of love that may or may not be correct. We also like to equate love with certain emotional feelings and therefore miss some of the more demanding sides of love, particularly the demand for caring for those in need who often cannot return our generosity. We also do well to note that authentic love is a faithful love. It extends beyond isolated moments of solidarity. We might say that there are many shapes and forms of Christian love. There will likewise be many configurations of Church life or, as theologians put it today, "ecclesial" life.

Out of the documents of Vatican II we can designate at least *five* ongoing expressions of ecclesial life in the Church. They range from a description of the Church universal to that of the smallest, most intense form of the Church, the Christian family. The Council called it "the domestic Church."[1]

It might be worthwhile to present a brief description of each form of ecclesial life that the Council mapped, because one will then have a better sense of the specific ecclesial situation of the Christian family.

In the spirit of Vatican I the meaning and value of the Church as a *universal* body was brought out in Vatican II. Of particular importance was the emphasis on the full stature of each and every member of the People of God. While it showed a proper appreciation of the diversity of roles or ministries in the Church, the Council sought first of all to state with absolute clarity that within the Church we are all important, as the fullness of the Church's life is accomplished only with the generous contributions of every member.

A second form of the Church, which was somewhat new in our ecclesial consciousness, was the designation of the national Church. These national bodies were to serve as mediating structures between the Church universal and the diocesan Church. This was a very realistic distinction. It was a recognition of the importance of cultural and regional uniqueness. It showed that the Church possesses a keen sense of the human side of ecclesial life. Also, the processes by which the national conferences run, their open elections and discussions, the effort toward collaborative ministry, their ability to organize special efforts to meet pressing needs in specific locales signal a promising development in the Church's sense of its own identity. In the next chapter we will describe the outstanding move made by the national conference of bishops in the United States in its adoption of a sensitive and enlighted pastoral strategy to deal with the manifold area of family life. The conference's leadership in the area of family-life ministry may prove to be the most significant contribution made by the Church of the United States ever to the Church universal.

[1]The Dogmatic Constitution on the Church (*Lumen Gentium*), section 11.

A third form of ecclesial life is that of the diocese. While the diocese has long enjoyed ecclesial status, Vatican II made it a point again to emphasize its role, as the fullness of Christ's power is made available though the person of the bishop. Of special importance was the *pastoral* emphasis given to the bishop's role in the Church. His leadership in overseeing and facilitating the pastoral efforts of the diocese, his role as primary celebrant of the liturgy, his personal expression of solicitude for the hurts of his people—all these designations serve again to emphasize that the Church must before all else be the continuation of Christ's presence among us. The Church's business is that of God, not that of human enterprise. This comes out most clearly in the discussion of the diocese and the role of the bishop in Vatican II.

The fourth communal structure singled out by the Council fathers was the local Church. Again there are noteworthy aspects to this move. What comes to the forefront is the importance of the parish liturgy, particularly its celebration of the Eucharist. The local Church, which is usually the parish community, is the common form of the Church most people think of when asked about *their* church. In the history of the Catholic Church in the United States, the parish was many things to many people. It often served as their point of contact with their new home in America, if they had recently arrived. It was the locale of their major educational experiences. If asked to retell the story of the their personal religious development, most Catholics would mention quite often their various experiences in the parish community. For them the parish was the concrete embodiment of their sense of being a Catholic Christian. The parish for better or worse made *real* what Christianity stood for.

In its discussion of the fifth form of authentic ecclesial communities, Vatican II reactivated a traditional description of the Christian family that was present in the early centuries of the Church, particularly in the writings of St. John Chrysostom. The Council called the Christian family a domestic Church or the Church of the home. There has been much made of this description particularly in the writings of the Popes since the Council. Paul VI used this designation often. His most well-known application came in his profound pastoral exhortation "On Evangelization in the

Modern World."[2] It is worth quoting him here to emphasize the force of this manner of defining the Christian family. Paul writes: "This means that there should be found in every Christian family the various aspects of the entire Church."

Paul VI is referring to the various dimensions of the Christian life present in the Church as a whole. The family is truly an evangelizing community, a worshiping community and a ministerial community. This establishes a foundation for the development of a whole theological understanding of family of incredible significance. While it may be true that the Christian family, in general, has yet to sense and appreciate its outstanding calling, there can be no doubt that a promising dogmatic foundation for a renewed theology of the Christian family has been laid. We might also recall the address quoted in the beginning of this book from John Paul I, where he also identified the Christian family as the domestic Church. The final chapters of our inquiry into the relation of the Church and family life will develop how "the various aspects of the entire Church" are present in the life of the Christian family.[3]

A theology of marriage and family life will be gained through the careful and honest examination of the human experiences inherent in that life, coupled with a truthful telling of the Christian story in relation to those experiences. As has been mentioned, it will be an expression of the life of "Church" in the home. It will be a description of how the reality of the Christian mystery, God's merciful and faithful love of humanity, of each one of us, impregnates the utterly personal life of marriage and the family. It will describe, in terms understandable to those who live the reality, the incredible friendship that God makes possible between humans because they are empowered to do so by his own companionship.

Christian marriage and family life is a special way of living those common human relationships. It is a realization, perhaps quite dim, that the relational events, which are created by the love of the marriage partners and their children, are a response to their appreciation of God's love and express *in* those human relationships their own response to God's love. In loving each other, in

[2] *Evangelii Nuntiandi*, section 71.
[3] *Ibid.*

accepting each other for better or worse, in fidelity and commitment, the family members demonstrate in quite earthly ways their
fundamental relationship with God. This love is a mystery, in the
words of the Epistle to the Ephesians, because it is rooted in the
mystery of God's own love made tangible in Jesus as he gave his
own life completely for others. Christian marital and family love
exist only because God's love is real, is accepted and understood,
however partially, by certain persons chosen by God to bear the
special weight of his love in human form. This choosing by God is
sometimes called the vocation to marriage.

At the foundation of Christian marital and family love is the
Church's covenant bond with God. None of these relational bonds
exist because of a forceful entry of one person into the life of
another. They are all based on freedom, and their continued life
depends on nourishment and cultivation. They ought never to be
taken for granted. There are, however, trust factors that can be
counted on no matter what. We can trust God to hold up this side
of the relationship. He has shown how far he would go with and
for us when he climbed the hill where his cross was planted. He
will never resist giving us what is absolutely best for us and our
relational life. Of course, this is often difficult to accept, but his
ways may not be our own. This has to be faced quite squarely
because we often select what is easy, comfortable and secure. But
these are not the life-giving virtues of a deep relational life, and it
is that deep life of sharing the incredible gift of life and love that
is played out daily in Christian family life.

In describing the Christian dynamics of marital life we must
consider the religious significance as touching more than simply
the wedding ceremony. The grace-empowered activity of Christian
marriage is operative *throughout* the life of the marriage. We may
want to limit "religion" to that event in the Church building, but
this would be a horrible distortion of the fundamental Christian
meaning of marriage and family life because the on-going events
of the home give sacramental meaning to marriage. While
the so-called Church building may be miles from the home, the site
where so much of the Christian life is being celebrated and
expressed is that other Church, the life of a marriage and family.

So far we have been emphasizing the *relational* life of the family as the context for Christian meaning. This has to be stated over and over to counteract the philosophy of individualism that was described in the last chapter. Likewise our description of the kind of love in the family has to be spelled out to distinguish it from what parades as love in the pop culture of America. That approach to love speaks primarily about emotional feelings, "turn-ons" and all that love can do for *me* when I fall into its grasp. It is a very passive type of experience. It happens to me when I don't expect it, and it departs with the same unpredictability. It's like a force, a power, a mysterious visitor who enters our life for a time, but cannot be trusted to remain forever. In a word, it is quite adolescent!

This is not to downplay emotional life. The point here is simply to make us aware of a much deeper kind of love—one which can truly knock us off our feet because it involves *everything* that we are. It is a total event. It enlarges us because we step out of our own narrow world into that of another. The pop culture's view of love turns us inward; Christian love opens us outward—so much so that it includes that mysterious One who stands at the foundation of the Universe and who is deeply our friend as well. Our love-life with God is pulled into our love-life with each other. That is the fundamental reason why pop love is so incomplete. It is too small, too petite, too trivial. It can contain only a small part of ourselves. It also restricts our growth into adulthood and into adult relationships.

In later chapters we will spell out some of the concrete implications of the Christian life for married and family persons. Here we are laying foundations. They must be strong because the building is intended to be mighty.

We are invited to make present the love of God in human form. This takes place *in* the relationships in the family and *in* the relationships of the family to outsiders. These can all be sacramental relationships. They flow from the sacramentality of the Church and the special gifts given to married Christians through the sacrament of Matrimony. These are charisms, extraordinary gifts given by God, that qualify the recipients as ministers of the Lord, true disciples of the living Lord who remains alive especially through their many expressions of generosity, care and service.

In the tradition of the Church, Christian marrriage has been described as having two purposes: the development of the love relationship between the marriage partners and the procreation of new life. These were best understood as being related purposes that reached their fullest expression in procreative love. The basic attitude of loving another was judged so great that that same love brought into existence, with the cooperation of God, new life. The ordinary expression of marital life in sexual intercourse took on a profound significance when joined with this Christian perspective.

Again we raise an issue that will often come into conflict with the views present in popular culture. A debate now rages in our land over the question: are we becoming an anti-children society? Of course the question has to be posed in such a way that the *real* intentions and values of people come to the surface. Surveys that ask: if you had it to do all over again, would you . . . have fewer children than you now have? Have no children at all? These questions yield answers that are sometimes disturbing. In general, they point to a growing attitude that children are undesirable and unnecessary parts of life. This is not merely based on whether people like children or not. It seems more the case that people want to live their own lives with the least amount of external interference. There are, no doubt, many reasons behind this apparent shift in values. Greater affluence, more ease of travel, more attractions outside the home all contribute to a person wanting these instead of something or someone else. Also, the basic cost of raising children is a factor of no small proportions. People do not seem very optimistic about the economic future and it is not difficult to find ample reasons for their worry.

Nevertheless, the question must be raised about our fundamental attitude toward the procreation of new life. How do we view our responsibilities to later generations? In our chapter discussing the human factors affecting family life, there was mention of the concern for the immediate, our preference for today's gusto. If we join this to the desire simply to fulfill ourselves, we clearly have a foundation for a narrow view of life and not much reason for generating new life. To be a bit cynical for a moment, perhaps if everyone in the world were that way, neither you nor I would choose to enter that world. What we are discussing here clearly touches upon some very basic matters. Of course, it must be noted that we do not all feel that way about new life. There is in fact widespread concern for the procreation, the protection and the nurturing of new life. What is recent, however, is that those who adopt this view have a gnawing feeling that there is not an extensive acceptance of their perspective.

So this stand carries with it today some sense of heroism. It cannot be argued that those who freely and lovingly bring children into the world are unaware of the enormous costs, both personal and financial, in living out their conviction. Theirs is not a blind love, but a love which knows that both risk and hope must be included in mature love. Their love is responsible, but it is also generous. It refuses to be paralyzed by incessant calculation or prevented from action simply because of a fear of the unknown future.

The Christian family gives witness to a view of life that is both beautiful and strange. Its values spring from the same well that Jesus drew from to give drink and life to the Samaritan woman. Theirs is a vision that was neither fashioned on Madison Avenue nor in the halls wherein were penned the founding documents of our country. Theirs is a vision that originates in a presence and power supporting our every breath and heartbeat. For God too is a power of love and life. And that is why when the Christian family understands itself, it also understands its Lord. It is a vision that comes from Jesus and through the community which remains faithfully bound to his spirit.

In our day, when the vision is not widely known or supported by the general culture, it is all the more necessary that the Church invest itself with the responsibility of supporting the Christian life of the family. The survival of the Christian family cannot be taken for granted, just as nothing that significant should ever be so treated. It is not so much the case that matters have come to such a desperate condition—although these do not seem to qualify as the best of times—that a special pastoral effort is called for to support Christian family life. The issue is deeper than that. It is deeper than what might be pointed to by pessimistic statistics. It is simply the fact that it is fitting and proper and wholly just that the Church do all it can for the Christian family (John Paul I).

And so on May 3, 1978, the National Conference of Catholic Bishops of the United States voted in formal session to approve a comprehensive pastoral strategy to support the life and spirit of the Christian family. The fundamental blueprint of this response is contained in "The Plan of Pastoral Action for Family Ministry: A Vision and Strategy." This will now be presented and analyzed. In many ways it is a document of great wisdom and creativity.

Chapter Four

INSIGHTS INTO THE PLAN FOR FAMILIES

WHAT FOLLOWS ARE SOME comments on the significance and the nature of the bishops plan for families of the Catholic Church in the United States. The reader is strongly advised to read the plan itself. Fortunately the United States Catholic Conference has published an excellent edition of the text, along with a selection of recent papal and episcopal texts dealing with family life. There is also a discussion guide and a listing of the key concepts of the plan. It can be ordered directly from the Publications Office, U.S.C.C., 1312 Massachussets Ave. N.W., Washington, D.C., 20005.

What must be mentioned first is that the plan is an enabling document. It is one of those "structures that facilitate" mentioned in the plan itself. Whether the plan will work or not depends entirely on the effort of the total Church to see that it is implemented right down to the grass roots. The *only* criteria for success will be where families themselves are enabled more effectively to reach their full Christian potential.

This also means that the plan is not a plan in the ordinary sense. It is not a formula for a set of required activities. It does not provide a detailed method for families to live by. It does give direction, but it is very open-ended as to where the final goal or set of goals might be situated. About all that can be said in a definitive way is that it gives a dynamic *framework* a *process,* and a *spirit* to the whole effort of developing family ministry. The ones who will give final form to the plan are the families themselves and they will have to be consulted in a special way.

The tone of the plan is more invitational than demanding. It leaves room for creativity and for the uniqueness of the many families in the Church. In a word, it truly *respects* the families that it intends to serve. It acknowledges their integrity as full members of the Church. It is saying to families: you tell us about yourself and where your strength is so that the Church can support you more; tell us where your weakness is so that the Church can also minister to you there. It is designed to assist families in the discovery of their own Christian abundance. This should indeed come as welcome news to those who are accustomed to hear the Church more readily point to their weaknesses and faults than to their strengths and virtues. The plan will present difficulty to those who find it more easy to condemn or are uneasy about pointing to the good in another.

As the plan is implemented, it will be more and more difficult to distinguish sharply between leaders and followers, but that is as it should be. Recall one of the fundamental insights of Vatican

II: the Church is, first of all, the People of God. Under that description the Council fathers wanted to acknowledge our equality before God. God is our only Lord; we are *all* disciples. While this understanding can be traced back to the very origins of the Church, it would have to be said that it was not always applied in practice. Of course, this is an extremely complex issue that has historical, cultural, educational and spiritual factors all intertwined to create the kind of Church we have today.

It is apparent, however, both from the developments in the more recent theologies of the Church, as well as from a description of actual practice in the contemporary Church, that there is more of a shared sense of ministry and responsibility. Because this issue is so pertinent to the relation of the Church to family life, our next chapter will treat this topic at length.

Perhaps more than any previous pastoral strategy that was created with the *whole* Church in mind, the plan for families really envisages a major role for the laity. After all, the bottom line for success will be determined primarily in terms of what happens on their turf. Yet it would be inappropriate to conclude that this is a plan *only* for the laity. The present leadership structures of the Church deserve respect and notice because a vital role in the plan will clearly be played by *all* the ecclesial structures that we described in the last chapter. Of particular importance will be the role of the parish priest. The plan mentions the need for special educational programs for the clergy, both priests and deacons, for religious and seminarians in all those matters touching its vision and strategy. Realistically, they will be the ones who often get matters started. They will also be entrusted with much of the educational responsibility for communicating to their people the Christian insights into marriage and family life. Though not exclusively, the local clergy will be a major factor in preparing couples for Christian marriage and in meeting their specific spiritual needs as their marriage and family life develop. The plan gives, in other words, a tremendous opportunity to develop a *team approach* to Christian ministry. It gives all Christians a common focus for the further development of the Lord's Kingdom on earth.

To gain a deeper understanding of where the plan fits into

the life of the Church today, it is important to note some of the key events that preceded its eventual unanimous approval by the National Conference of Catholic Bishops. Those events took place rather quickly, which means that those not abreast of developments might have difficulties appreciating all the ramifications of the plan itself.

It began in 1975 when the bishops, who were then members of the administrative board of the United States Catholic Conference, noted the spiraling divorce rate and wondered whether the various crises affecting families might be related to other problems in the Church. At that time it was simply a pastoral concern, but the bishops felt that the question should be pursued through an organized investigation. It was decided that there should be created a special commission to look into the question. Subsequently there was then gathered a group of seven bishops from around the country, the twelve diocesan regional representatives of diocesan family-life offices, a group of scholars representing the human and theological sciences, and other persons who had a particular knowledge or competence in the area of marriage and family life. In all there were forty members invited to serve on what came to be called the U.S.C.C. *ad hoc* Commission on Marriage and Family Life.

The commission met three times over a period of a year and a half. Its meetings were characterized by an honest and frank exchange among the participants. As is apparent from the forty-five proposals, which were submitted at the conclusion of their meetings, the commission's work was also characterized by rigor and directness. The final report of the commission is available through the Department of Education of the United States Catholic Conference. One of the recommendations of the commission was the enactment of a comprehensive pastoral plan for marriage and family-life ministry. When the commission prioritized its proposals, the plan was voted number one!

It should also be mentioned that the other forty-four proposals are in the process of being implemented as well. The work of the commission was so thorough that it truly created an exhaustive, far-reaching set of pastoral areas for the Church's consideration and response for many years to come. An example of the timetable for these many proposals: in the plan itself, after two years of preparation are complete, the Church will embark on a ten-year period of research and development for family life. It is even appropriate to ask whether a decade is sufficient, or whether it might be better simply to admit that family-life ministry will be an essential part of Church life for both the short- and long-range future.

In addition to the work of the *ad hoc* commission, two other consultations were taking place in 1976. There was first the Bicenntenial hearing which was labeled "The Call to Action." The purpose of that hearing was to bring to the surface the major concerns in the Church, particularly in areas dealing with peace and justice. When the approximately 800,000 responses were finally tabulated, the issues that covered family directly, and those that stemmed from the relation of the Church to the family, accounted for the largest number of specific concerns.

It is also worth noting that those areas most commonly mentioned became part of the plan approved by the bishops. It was their attempt to meet the expressed needs of the Church. Perhaps the most telling response in the Call to Action was the common feeling that families did not sense the *support* of the Church for their basic values of family life. Families felt that they were not understood by the institutional Church. Good families establish high goals for themselves. Their efforts to be good marriage partners, good parents and good providers, and all that this responsibly entails, were often felt to be an orientation that was *only* supported *in* the family. The various institutions outside the family—the state, the media, and even the Church—appeared indifferent to these family concerns.

Families also asked the Church for help in teaching basic Christian values in the home. They asked for guidance in creating meaningful home-prayer activities. They were also concerned about passing on their family traditions. What should be noted, then, is the *isolation* experienced by families, a sense that whatever is done by the family had to be done alone. From the human standpoint, this is certainly not a healthy state of affairs, because that which is done alone and unsupported will eventually be questioned and perhaps abandoned, particularly if it is at odds with what is popularly done in the wider society.

It is particularly tragic given the fact that the Christian community should be, at a minimum, a support group for its members. No Christian should ever feel isolated, particularly when it is a matter of commonly held values and practices that have a meaningful relationship to the fundamental spirit of Christianity.

What seems to be happening is a state of affairs that is all too common in contemporary society: a breakdown of significant and supportive ties in all basic communities larger than the nuclear family. That this happens widely does not give the Church a license simply to submit to the situation. By creating meaningful community in all types of situations the Church may, in fact, create one of its more significant counter-cultural moves in seriously and vigorously resisting this trend toward the erosion of relational ties. It should be added that this is certainly being done already in a few pockets of ecclesial life. Many of the so-called movements within the Church are basically attempts at creating meaningful Christian community. Here we might single out the charismatic movement, Marriage Encounter and the Christian Family Movement, the Family-Cluster movement and the Cursillo movement. While the religious base of each of these movements may be different, they share one trait in common: they are designed to create a community of support for the enthusiasm they feel for the Christian life.

A second consultation, which took place in 1976, was that of listening to those formally involved in the family-life apostolate throughout the country. Twelve hearings were chaired by Father Donald Conroy, the U.S.C.C. Family Life representative, resulting in the surfacing of 155 specific needs for serious consideration in the Church. Heading that list were issues like that of the ministry to divorced and separated Catholics. Other significant issues mentioned were the need for dealing with the women's movement, particularly as it influences family life; the need for a meaningful theology of marriage, family and sexuality; the issue of permanency of commitment in marriage and family and the need to develop and support effectively leaders in family ministry.

There were, therefore, three significant resources available in the Church so that it could formulate a realistic agenda for supporting Christian family life. The plan is a first step to embody that move. It must be remembered that it is *only* a first step. It should not be given a meaning that was never intended.

What became so apparent in the various consultations was that no single area, no single issue surfaced as totally dominant and that, therefore, no single solution should be attempted to meet the complex needs of family life. What resulted, then, was a very broad attempt to cover a wide range of areas. In the plan this was described as the effort to create a pastoral vision and strategy for *total* family ministry. This can be shown clearly by referring to the six target areas of ministry that are described in the plan itself. A summary of these six spheres of ministry will provide a meaningful understanding of what total family ministry signified.

AREA 1: MINISTRY FOR PRE-MARRIEDS AND SINGLES

It is now clear that success in marriage and family life is not simply related to what happens after the wedding ceremony. We all bring into our marriages a personal history of family living that extends back to our own birth—and before! Therefore, in any attempt to create a realistic ministry for family life, one can never begin too soon. To be sure, this area of the plan will focus on all programs of marriage preparation, which must also be constantly updated and improved. The programs will cover ministry to those at the threshold of marriage (proximate preparation), as well as those still at some distance from marriage (remote preparation). This area will encompass formal programs, which will ordinarily be presented in a school, retreat house or rectory context, and those that informally occur in the home. It must always be remembered that most of what the plan includes will take place *primarily* in the home, the heart of the domestic Church.

A significant inclusion is the ministry to singles. It is often a valid complaint of singles that they are the forgotten members of society. Their grievance is particularly pertinent in Church life where the sense of family, though not all of what it might be, is at least more evident than is the sense of singles. What deserves pastoral attention then is that singles often live as family persons, perhaps not in the biological sense of that term, but in the sense of belonging to and being accepted by a community of friends. Certainly we should never fall into the condition of considering family with only a narrow definition. Family should be viewed, at least in part, as a *functional* reality that provides a sense of attachment and loyalty to persons whatever their social situation. We all need some type of family. This need arises from both human and Christian existence. The ministry to singles is intended also to touch those who are middle-aged and advanced in years as well.

AREA 2: MINISTRY FOR MARRIED COUPLES

While it may appear that a primary goal of family-life ministry would, in fact, be the enrichment of the relationship between the wife and husband, it remains true that except for some rather recent developments, e.g., Marriage Encounter, this has not hitherto been the case. Very little was done in the Church to assist couples in their intimate relational life. There were fortunately available in some locales counseling services as well as occasional retreats for married couples, and if such couples were in the right place at the right time, they may have heard a lecture or two about marital enrichment.

Of course, there may have not been a strongly felt need for such programs. Perhaps the stresses on the marital relationship were not as devastating as they are today. We can only speculate at length on possible reasons for this blind spot in the Church's ordinary ministerial services. Here it is more worthwhile to speak of the need *today* for this assistance. Clearly, the survival of marital love in the contemporary world cannot be taken for granted. It must be understood, nourished and supported if it is to remain strong.

Earlier we spoke of the development of good theological descriptions of the Christian life that support a deep relational love between wife and husband. At least theoretically, marital love is prized in the Christian community. The need for honest communication and mutual support, for a shared life that covers *all* the areas of human development—the physical, the intellectual, the emotional and the spiritual—all this is without question something desired in the Church. What is needed however is a clear understanding of all that is entailed in these many areas of development. Might the Church unconsciously be responsible for impairing growth in some or all of these areas? The plan calls for research. It mandates that the Church listen to the real words of married couples. It calls on the Church to be pro-marriage!

AREA 3: MINISTRY FOR PARENTS

If you have ever wondered whether parenting was a difficult task, just ask a parent, any parent. Next to the weather, parenting is probably the most discussed area of human experience. For many, it is an area of great stress in their lives. If you consult the experts for guidance in parenting, you will discover that there is a wide range of theories on how most effectively to parent. The reason for this is that our basic approach to the fundamental meaning of human and Christian life is always going to influence our philosophy of parenting. Since there are so many philosophies of life available in the marketplace, you can be sure that there will be an abundant number of philosophies of parenting to choose from.

The parents play a unique role in the process of Christian formation. They are not only the first religious educators of their children, but they are also probably the most influential. Of course, it is very difficult to map the influence of parents. It is so deep and widespread that you will find it difficult to chart where it begins and where it ends, where it starts and where it stops. The influence will also be difficult to define because it becomes a part of the very person of the child. In their hearts parents know this, and that is why their concern for the quality of their relationship with their children is viewed with such concern and sometimes anxiety.

Adding to the complexity of parenting is that what might be called the common structure of parenting—a mother and father as more or less lifelong parents of a particular child—is diminishing every year. Single parents, stepparents, adopted parents, parents who are divorced or separated from their marriage partners, widowed parents, part-time parents—the mixture of parenting situations is very real. Any programs designed to assist parents will have to take account of this pluralistic state of affairs.

Parents need and want help. This was a very common request in the Call to Action hearings. Special guidelines from the United States Catholic Conference are now available to assist those who would like to design creative and meaningful programs in Christian parenting. These programs will have to take account of the actual cultural conditions that make parenting today significantly different from what it was a few years ago. Just the influence of television alone would be enough to modify the situation quite profoundly. If this is doubted, ask a parent!

Ministry to parents will include educational programs for young and old. It will include a description of the various stages of human development. It will provide communication skills. It will assist parents in their role as those charged with the immediate witnessing and communication of the Christian Gospel to their children. It will also be a place where like-to-like ministry will be encouraged. Surely there is much basic Christian wisdom that is just waiting to be expressed and shared *in* the community. And it means much to know that the wisdom has been shown to work, because if the truth ever demanded practicality, parenting would be the place.

AREA 4: MINISTRY FOR DEVELOPING FAMILIES

The family is a social unit. Does this appear to be a totally obvious statement? The key word in the assertion is "unit." That concept contains the notions of unity, communality, wholeness and integrity. On paper it is relatively simple to affirm family solidarity. In actual fact, it is an accomplishment of no small effort. The survival of the family as a social unit can no longer be taken for granted, at least if we focus on a particular family. It is a much different question if we simply examine the survival of the family. Occasionally an apocalyptic-minded sociologist will announce its demise so as to capture a momentary headline, but the anthropological fact is too widely established: there has always been some kind of family arrangement. Nevertheless, it is still a struggle for the individual family. And the pressures against its enduring are of an unprecedented magnitude.

There is an old axiom in the theology of the spiritual life: if you are not progressing, you are regressing. Somewhat the same can be said for Christian family life. Thus, the area of ministry for families themselves is called ministry to *developing* families. If the family is not experiencing growth, if its relational life is not keeping pace with the ordinary sense of maturation, if the family is not continuously adjusting to the ever new needs of its members, then it will have a sense of regression and atrophy. In its own way there will be a feeling of *rigor mortis*, and in a world of freedom and viable options, the individual members will simply turn elsewhere for their fundamental interpersonal ties. This sometimes spells divorce. It sometimes means simply a hardening of the arteries of communication and love within the family.

The ministry to developing families does not emphasize these negative elements because it is a ministry of enrichment. It is based on a belief in the inherent goodness and gifts of the family. It seeks simply to draw upon that reservoir of God-given and humanly enriched potential to produce an even greater expression of God's love in the human form of the family. It accepts the Christian family as a genuine form of the Church and ministers to that reality.

This ministry will appreciate the many shapes of the family. It will be sensitive to the special needs that surface in young families, of families in their middle years, and of families in their golden years. It will also move toward the greater activization of the ministerial capabilities of families themselves. We perhaps have grown so accustomed to viewing the family as a composite of individual members that we overlook the family in its integral wholeness. And this disregard for family solidarity brings us to speculate whether social realities of some duration have any meaning in our society. The question is not whether relational life is possible, but rather whether that relational life is also characterized by fidelity and unconditional commitment. Is it really possible to say "forever" to someone? Or are we limited to relationships that burn with a short fuse?

From a Christian standpoint there is a frightening importance embedded in this line of questions. Throughout the biblical tradition one of the most difficult dimensions to grasp was God's fidelity to his promises and to his people as his friends. The prophets had to repeat over and over that the Lord remained with his people through both thick and thin. The Lord had an *everlasting* covenant with his people, a pledge of companionship that knew no limits.

This matter of the fidelity of the Lord did not simply remain a theoretical concern. If it was to be communicated effectively, it had to become a part of human history. Fidelity had somehow to be embodied in human relationships. From time to time certain persons were invited to express that fidelity in a certain way. Hosea was asked to rejoin his unfaithful wife, Gomer, as a sign of God's forgiving fidelity.

The Lord "tested" Israel's commitment so as to draw from his people an even stronger devotion, because the more they gave of themselves to him, the more they would find their deepest fulfillment. This was not easy to explain. The Book of Job is the best example of the attempt to wrestle with the issue. In the end all one can do is stand before the One who was there when the foundations of the universe were laid, and confess trust in his wisdom.

But there remain more chapters to the story of God's faithfulness. It is one thing to observe from a distance the trials and tribulations of a friend. It is something quite different to join the friend and truly share his or her situation. So the Lord took on flesh. God became one of us and lived and died among us to convince us once and for all that he was *with* us. It was not so much that he was never with us, but that he was with us in *that* way. He would remain bound to us in a relationship so deep that theologians would say that he is closer to us than we are to ourselves. And this intimacy would last forever!

The reality of God's incredible bond with us should be expressed in human form and in human relationships. That is where Christian marriage and family life enter the picture. The relational life of the home is empowered by God to embody in human form his faithful love. It takes effort for this to become a part of Christian family life. It needs the assistance and support of the Christian community. It needs that expression of ministry which is termed in the plan "ministry to developing families." This ministry will aim at making available the human and Christian resources required for the creation and development of the Christian family. Given this mighty goal, the Church may have to rearrange its pastoral priorities quite decisively. It will have to embark on an investigation to determine what's needed by families for their own Christian enrichment. It will have to learn about those riches already present in the family that may be asleep. It will have to ask whether the ordinary ministerial life of the Church really supports the development of the Christian family. It will have to ask whether the Church really comes across as pro-family. Is a family sense a major consideration in liturgical planning, in parish scheduling, in the social life of the local community, in the educational operation of the parish—in everything?

AREA 5: MINISTRY FOR HURTING FAMILIES

Health care is usually divided into preventative care and the care that heals. In family ministry we can speak of a ministry that enriches family life by building on the strengths already present— "ministry to developing families"—and a ministry that seeks to heal the many wounds that result from family disharmony, the physical, psychological or social problems that afflict family life. Disharmony may at times simply be the "growing pains" that inevitably accompany human and relational development. From time to time, we all need healing because we are born into a condition of hurt. As families, we will likewise experience moments or even years of hurt. In response to that need, the plan points to a special area of family ministry, that of "ministry to hurting families."

In many ways the Church has engaged in a ministry to hurting families for a long time. Sometimes this took the form of the establishment of counseling services staffed by professional personnel. Sometimes, it simply meant the pastoral care of a sensitive priest or religious to individuals or families in need of support, advice, prayer or just a person to talk to. These expressions of ministerial concern, however, were often given on the fringe of the Church's ordinary life. Professional services in a Church setting were meager. And while the priest was commonly approached in marital or family problems, his own feelings of inadequacy and an overextension of his own personal resources prevented his help from being all that it might be.

In recent years there have been some promising breakthroughs in the Church's ministry to hurting families. There has been a greater concern for providing professional services for individuals and families, especially through Catholic Charities or other expression of social services. Some of this effort has reached to the parish level in an imaginative and promising program called "parish outreach." Diocesan family-life offices often provide skilled counselors for marriage partners and families in need of their help.

Perhaps one of the most interesting new areas of development is in the training of married couples, as paraprofessional counselors. They are given special training for dealing with many of the ordinary problems of family life. They learn what they can do and where their range of effective competency ends, which is the time they must refer their "case" to someone with more developed skills. Most of these couples serve on a parish level. They demonstrate that there will exist on the local scene all kinds of untapped ministerial potential. By being invited to serve, and by being given a modicum of training, they are able to serve within the community in a manner consonant with their calling and within the range of their indigenous talents. It is also a form of like-to-like ministry. There is a special value in a couple assisting another couple. They will often be able to speak of crossing the same terrain.

Counseling or assistance in general is not simply for the down-and-outers but can be an ordinary strategy to be used from time to time in Christian family life. We can learn from the better strategies of the health-care professions that we should avail ourselves of services before a situation develops to a critical level. In family life, we will all hurt occasionally. For the Church the challenge is to free people to be able to ask for help, and to facilitate their healing by providing adequate resources in the local community where such help is easily identified and used. It will be that community's way of saying that the Lord's care and concern for the sick, the blind, the weak and the oppressed remain present in the caring persons of that community.

AREA 6: MINISTRY FOR LEADERSHIP COUPLES AND FAMILIES

If the plan develops as most communal projects in the Church do, the effort toward achievement will be concentrated in a few families who will serve as the vanguard for the movement. Ideally, the total community would be activated, but realism forewarns us against such hopes. The privilege and the burden will fall on only a few. And they will have special needs, given their role with its many taxing dimensions. One of these is the strain on one's own family life once one becomes involved in helping others. Leadership and participation in family ministry flows from a relatively new sense of Church. Those who enter the field will have a sense of being trailblazers. They will find, as did the pioneers of old, that you cannot count on there being a Holiday Inn every few miles along the road. There may be some hard times.

The Church ought then not to forget its family-life ministers. To detail all their needs is impossible. We must, however, begin the discussion of where family ministers fit into the life of the Church, because as we develop greater insight into who they are, we will be in a better position to ask what they need. The topic is so important that the entire next chapter will consider this issue.

Chapter Five

LEADERSHIP IN
FAMILY MINISTRY

I KNOW WHAT IT IS UNTIL you ask me to define it. That was the response given by St. Augustine to the person who asked him to define "time." Much the same can be said about the concept of leadership. Not only is the term difficult to define, it is also a designation that many Church persons find uncomfortable, especially if it is applied to them. Perhaps we unknowingly carry the impression that a leader will tend to be dictatorial, oppressive or even arrogant, but of course there are countless leaders who are genuinely humble and responsive to the needs of the community. Naturally, there are dictators too.

The Church has had its own history of leadership. It has had its periods of positive and creative leadership, as well as its moments of indecisive, even corrupt guidance. The question as to who are the *real* leaders in the Church is also part of the issue. We can speak of those who are leaders by ordination or by appointment. But there are also those who lead simply by example, by living the kind of life that inspires others to be more virtuous, more generous, more considerate, more alive. They would be more like the leaven in the loaf that the Lord described as being so necessary for the life of the Kingdom. The leaven is unnoticed, so much a part of the dough that is is indistinguishable from the mass of ingredients. Yet without it, the bread would be flat.

Leadership in the Church community must be defined in Christian terms, not in models drawn from the world of politics. Christian leadership is born from the power of God, not from potency created and driven by human interest or ambition. God may well use created talents and gifts, but God may just as commonly overlook those persons natively talented to empower the weak. In other words, there will forever be a certain mystery about Christian leadership. No one can say beforehand that he or she is not the leadership-type because their resources are not simply their own. The whole history of God's chosen people is sprinkled with examples of those who felt the restrictions of personal inadequacy when faced with the challenges of leadership. And it is well to experience that sense of insufficiency, because what we are invited to accomplish is well beyond the range of simple human achievement. The genuine Christian leader is to assist the Spirit in the renewal of the face of the earth. The realization of the New Creation in human society and in the lives of individual persons is, in part, accomplished through the generous response of those willing to take the lead, those who risk speaking out the truth, and those who find vested in them the strength to support others in their struggle to live a full human and Christian life.

Are we saying, then, that the Christian community will be

constituted by some who are the leaders, and by others who are the followers? Do the many references to the shepherd and the sheep validate that kind of communal structure? The answer, perhaps surprising to some, is a straightforward "no." This answer, of course, must be explained because we are touching a very sensitive and delicate area of theological and ecclesial discussion. Wrapped up in the issue of leadership is the question of the very meaning of being a Christian!

To its great credit the Second Vatican Council provided us with a very rich understanding of the Church. Following the insights of Paul in his first letter to the Corinthians, the Council described the Church as a community of profuse and bountiful diversity. Its richness was the result of the many gifts and talents invested in each member by the creative Spirit of God. It was the task of the community to respect and support the full expression of that diversity. Some were empowered as teachers, others as those who could discern well, some were gifted healers, others were inspired as prayer leaders.

The Church was to be a community of encouragement and support, a place where the dignity and significance of each and every member were both acknowledged and respected. There exists in each of us an incredible potential to do good, but it awaits both the call of God and the prompting of the community. The community becomes more active as the dynamics of the many relationships within it serve to stimulate each person. Each member has a unique contribution to make toward enriching the life of the community, yet part of its activization depends on the stimulation of others. We are called forth, like Abraham, from where we lived in security and contentment to a new place in the community. We are invited to a new level of participation. We are summoned to be a full and accomplished member of the community. We are recognized as an adult.

It was in this spirit that the opening sections of the Dogmatic Constitution on the Church, *Lumen Gentium*, were fashioned at Vatican II. The Church was described as the People of God, as a community of free and responsible persons with a fundamental equality before God. This stature of equality also implied that the full range of responsibility fell to each Christian. It was the intent of the Council's description of the Church to call forth the participation of *all* its members. This did not imply, however, that we would all be doing the same thing or that we would all be involved in the same task.

Right after its affirmation of our shared equality, the Council spoke of the special and unique roles that each of us would exercise. Behind that affirmation was the vision that each of us is very special in God's view and that we are invited to express our uniqueness in the life of the Kingdom. Clearly, we are not clones!

Sometimes it is erroneously suggested that the Council documents paved the way for some kind of "lay takeover" of the Church. This is sometimes suggested in contemporary descriptions of the Church that speak of "the age of the laity" or that point to the waning of vocations to the priesthood or religious life. Such a view of the Church is not at all a part of the Council's vision of the Church.

What is at work is a vision of the charism of each Christian that must be respected and supported, along with an appreciation of the full range of contexts where the power of the Christian reality is to be felt. That range is coextensive with the totality of creation. It is particularly necessary to point to the complex and dynamic life of community and social justice as an area of decided ecclesial interest. The concern for peace and justice is not simply an afterthought to the Christianization of the world. Rather, this concern, in the words of the World Synod of Bishops that met to discuss the place of justice in the Christian life, is a constitutive part of the Gospel itself. The Good News is that we live in the light and power of a merciful God. This also means that we are enlightened and empowered to transform the world into a place where God's attitude of concern and care is manifest in the lives of those who are elected and named "Christians."

Even to begin the accomplishment of this incredible task, it will be necessary to call forth the fullest possible response of *all* Christians. It is, therefore, out of an appreciation of the many gifts and talents inherent in the Church, and out of a sense of the total range of created life which anticipates, so to speak, being brought into the Kingdom, that the Church now speaks of itself as a People of God: each member empowered and invited to exercise a vital and significant role in that undertaking. Once we realize the vastness of that challenge, there will be no question of "not enough work to go around." Nor will there be a question of individual Christians having to defend their ministerial "turf." Of course, this will not be a problem *if* we are able, as a community, to come to a workable designation of the proper area of ministerial compentency for the various "types" of ecclesial persons.

The Church appears to be in a transitional moment in this latter situation. Particularly for the Catholic Church in the United States there has been a rather heavy emphasis on the leadership role of the ordained clergy and the professed religious. For the most part their leadership has been accepted and taken for granted. There have been isolated examples of lay leadership (the Catholic Worker movement and the Christian Family Movement might be cited), but these were exceptions to what we might call the mainstream of Catholic life, particularly as it took shape in the local parish.

While there are, no doubt, meaningful historical reasons for leadership being almost exclusively vested in the clergy and religious, there are also reasons to call this pattern into question. It has already been mentioned that Vatican II presented a broader portrait of ecclesial life. It can also be argued that the tight pattern of leadership, where a few were named leaders and many were designated as followers, wrought harm on *both* classes.

The leaders were saddled with most of the responsibility, most of the anxiety generated by the inevitable shortcomings of the local community and, most sadly, a sizeable chunk of the blame for any lack of perfection in the community. It was at the feet of the pastor and his associates that the proverbial "buck" stopped.

The followers, known also as the laity, suffered because they were allowed to slip into patterns of dependency and insignificant involvement. They grew up in the belief that the Church belonged to the fathers just as they felt that the school was the domain of the nuns. We are all too familiar with this pattern. It needs no lengthy description. What is worth reflection, however, is how this designation of leadership sorely hurt both the leaders and the followers.

The times are now changing and in a manner that promises a significant alteration in our view of Church leadership. What seems to be coming, however, is not a *shift* of leadership, but an *expansion* of leadership to include, hopefully, the entire community!

What is also surfacing in Church life is the importance of shared leadership, which more aptly expresses the ministerial life of the ecclesial community. After the Council the first groups within the Church that took upon themselves the task of updating were the communities of women religious. Many of these communities went through a process of communal discernment more clearly to understand their particular spirit as a community and more effectively to plan for the future. What these communities learned was the value of genuine communal leadership. They learned that the insights, ideas and values of each member were a precious resource to be used in planning and in charting the direction for future ministerial activity. When it was time to move the community by decisive direction, the leadership that founded the move was the expression of the *whole* community.

A similar pattern has been used in Catholic dioceses and parishes. While the bishop or the pastor remains as the designated leader in making primary pastoral decisions, the *manner* in which those decisions are formulated will often include the participation of a significant segment of that community. Clearly this is a new style of leadership, although informed Church historians can certainly point to other periods of the Church when leadership by consensus was operative.

Why have we discussed leadership at such length? How does this topic relate to our overall concern for family life? The topic is important because unless the laity assume a *significant* leadership posture in the area of family ministry, this area of ministry will exist only as a sideline interest in the life of the Church. This is so because the laity are, for the most part, the family people of the Church. It is also because they possess the needed competencies in virtue of their Christian vocation as married and family persons in the Church.

To establish the theological basis for this claim, we will review a very significant section of the Dogmatic Constitution on the Church from Vatican II, the chapter on the meaning and role of the laity (Chapter IV). The laity are singled out for specific mention because "there are certain things which pertain in a particular way to the laity, both men and women, by reason of their situation and mission" (section 30).

This chapter of *Lumen Gentium* represents some of the most advanced thinking on the place of the laity in Church life. It is positive, supportive and challenging. Pastors are reminded to acknowledge the special gifts and services proper to the laity and to seek a community of cooperation that can best be described as a "common undertaking with one heart" (section 30). Clearly the intent of the Council was to emphasize that ministry is not a private accomplishment, but a movement of the *entire* community with each member doing his or her proper yet special task.

The proper realm of lay activity is that of the secular. But the secular is not to be understood as devoid of Christian salvific meaning. Quite the contrary, one of the most forceful messages of Vatican II was to emphasize the Christian significance of the world. While this is particularly the theme of the Pastoral Constitution on the Church in the Modern World, *Gaudium et Spes*, the value of Christian involvement in the secular is viewed throughout the Council documents as nothing less than an extension of the principle of the Incarnation, of God's great love for the world demonstrated conclusively in God becoming flesh. The Church is in the world to transform the world. The fundamental mission of the Church, as it continues the work of Christ in history, is the salvation of the *world*. Therefore, when the Council speaks of the laity's task as "in the world," this is by no means to be interpreted as a second-best or marginal consideration. It is the laity's proper and best contribution to the spread of God's Kingdom.

The words of the Council say it well:

But the laity, by their very vocation, seek the kingdom of God by engaging in temporal affairs and by ordering them to the plan of God. They live in the world, that is, in each and in all of the secular occupations. They live in the ordinary circumstances of family and social life, from which the very web of their existence is woven. (Section 32.)

None of this is said by concession or apology. Rather it is stated with dignity and importance. The laity are to "work for the sanctification of the world from within" (*Ibid.*). Their task is to assist the Spirit in *sanctifying*, which is not at all a denial of the secular nature of their effort. It is rather an affirmation of its proper finality in being building-blocks out of which the Kingdom of God is formed. It is also noteworthy that family life is specifically mentioned as part of the "web." The lay person is a gifted Christian who is empowered to be "a witness and a living instrument of the mission of the Church" (section 33). In other words, the lay person is a Church person as much as anyone else.

It is appropriate here to recall something that was mentioned at the very beginning of the book: that Christian family life is a genuine expression of the Church. It is part of the very life of the Church. The implications of this affirmation are clear. A most fitting domain of the lay apostolate will be family life!

How well the Council document on the Church states just that in concluding that the extraordinary power of the Gospel is capable of taking form in the daily social and family life of the laity! Through these structures, the laity evangelizes. They announce the presence and significance of Christ, by both their actions and their word, and their expression carries a special power and force because it comes from the everyday and ordinary moments of human life. The Council's words are both eloquent and meaningful:

In connection with this function [evangelization], that state of life which is sanctified by a special sacrament

is obviously of great value, namely, married and family life. For where Christianity pervades a whole way of life and ever increasingly transforms it, there will exist both the practice and an excellent school of the lay apostolate. In such a home, husband and wife find their proper vocation in being witnesses to one another and to their children of faith in Christ and love for Him. The Christian family loudly proclaims both the present virtues of the kingdom of God and the hope of a blessed life to come. (Section 35.)

Several salient insights can be found in this text. The family is described as a school for the apostolate of the laity. It is the seedbed where children learn the meaning of what it is to be a Christian. It is a starting place for the marriage partners' personal apostolic activity. It is their first "audience" for their own proclamation of the Gospel. Of course, this will not be done in a "churchly" manner, but in the ordinary expressions of acceptance, affirmation and support that ought to be part of the daily interaction of the Christian family.

The Christian family itself "loudly proclaims" the reality of Kingdom life, right here and now, as it also embodies hope in the eventual full arrival of the Kingdom of God. Its word is clearly credible because the message is forged out of living substance: the genuine reality of family life. The role of the Christian family in the fundamental task of spreading the Good News is surfacing as a major component in the Church's renewed commitment to evangelization. This topic deserves specific consideration. Later in this book (Chapter Eight) a full examination of the witness capacity of the Christian family will be offered.

A sign of the Christian maturity of the local Church will be its openness in both allowing and facilitating the full participation of the laity in the everyday and ordinary expressions of ecclesial life. The Church will demonstrate this openness particularly in listening to the prophetic word that comes from the laity, a word that discerns the presence and activity of the Spirit in the secular. The laity's word is certainly not the only word in the conversation of the Church. It will be a word that is blended with the word of the clergy and the religious in forming a total conversation. Just as healthy family life results from honest and open communication, so also will the life of the Church be enhanced when each is able truly to hear the other, and respond with honesty and concern. Leadership that is decisive and sensitive will arise from within the community, and it will be a leadership that is truly sacramental: the living Word of God will spring from the human gestures of community.

In the last decade the Church has begun to employ skills derived from the human sciences designed to foster leadership development and the formation of community. Motivational workshops, management seminars, sensitivity sessions and organizational planning meetings are used in dioceses and parishes, often with great success. When these processes of development enter Church life, however, there is a danger that the methods or systems become more important than the fundamental reasons for their being used, which is the fuller actualization of the inherent capacities of the Christian community. There is also the danger that these methods appear as "brought down from above" or as just the most recent form of maintaining the dependency of the "followers," maybe not so much to a designated leader but to a designated system.

Leadership that is authentically "of the community" will inevitably have a messy character to it. It will lack the efficiency of a well-oiled machine because it will be the result of the rough-rubbing of real persons against one another. When each of us is free enough to state his or her real feelings, genuine views of how it is, agreements and disagreements, our meetings are apt to look more like a caucus of the Democratic party. Of course, someone will have the last word and in the Church provision is made for that need in terms of the role of the bishop and the pastor. What is being argued here, however, is that leadership is not theirs alone, but it is, according to the mind of Vatican II, a collegial leadership, a shared leadership, a corporate leadership. It respects the competencies of *all* the members of the community. It respects the full stature and adulthood of the membership. It knows of no other designation of Christian adulthood than that which is active, expressive, responsible and alive!

When it comes to matters dealing directly with family life and family ministry, the primary spotlight will shine on the leadership charism of married and family Christians. The discernment of the real exigencies of families will come from the expressions of families themselves. It should be mentioned that the suggested procedure for implementing the "Plan of Pastoral Action for Family Ministry" begins with the process of pastoral *listening*. It should also be added that the listening posture should not cease once a *plan* has been agreed to. It should be embedded in the ordinary practice of Christian ministry as an ongoing corrective process. It should be part of the style of *all* Christian ministry. Given the complexities of family life, the listening attitude should always be part of the pastoral agenda of family ministry.

Let us move this discussion one step further. Suppose that there have surfaced in a specific ecclesial community persons desiring to dedicate themself more fully to family ministry. This is not a hypothetical consideration, as there has developed over the years considerable participation in family ministry in the Catholic Church in the United States. It is not unheard of for a diocese to point to over a thousand volunteers involved in its various programs in family ministry. As the vision for families present in the bishops' plan becomes more widespread, the numbers of active participants will swell considerably. There must furthermore be a sense of the many uncounted participants who will never join a specific movement or be in a special diocesan or parish program, but who live the reality of family ministry in their own families. One might even argue that if we were able to count the number of genuine family ministers, they would far outnumber any other group of Christians who have a particular ministerial focus.

But such a census is impossible because, ironically, many Christians who are already deeply immersed in family ministry are not aware of that fact. They have not been "named" as ministers, and tragically their sense of being Christian does not include the common and everyday elements of their personal family life. Being named, designated or commissioned is an important part of developing a Christian awareness. The roots of "naming" are deep in the Christian reality. Being named by God as adopted child, as disciple and follower, as bearer of Christ and the Gospel are significant elements in developing a conscious awareness of all that we are.

It is part of the Church's responsibility to establish "rites of designation" where the individual member is assisted in the formulation of his or her particular sense of participation. The Church is recovering this sense in its commissioning of ministers of religious education. It should be extended creatively and meaningfully in the many areas of family ministry. It is clearly part of the needs of leadership.

This brings us to a most significant topic: the ministry for leadership couples and families. It is the sixth area of ministry mentioned in the bishops' plan. As stated in the plan itself, this area of ministry is so often overlooked! It is much like the dynamics of family life itself: we take each other for granted.

While in theory it has been argued that every member of the Church is a leader, we will nevertheless be faced with the situation that only some will live out that designation. Those who do step forward into active family ministry deserve not only the recognition and gratitude of the Church, they also deserve the care and support of the Church. And what must be respected above all else is *their own* family life!

While no detailed blueprint of ministry to the ministers is possible—local conditions and personal needs will always particularize the situation—some general direction might be given as to their care. A sample approach could be organized around the following needs of the family minister. They possess a need for: (1) recognition, (2) guidance, (3) enrichment, and (4) support.

First of all, they deserve recognition. This is the "naming" procedure that was already described. Family ministry is a specialized ministry in the Church. It is a most significant activity to the Lord, and that ought to be communicated to those involved in this ministry. One of the basic human needs is that of approval. We desire to know that what we do *counts*. This doesn't mean that we demand someone at our side giving us constant "stroking" or applause. We are adults and can operate quite effectively without exaggerated recognition. But we do need some. We need to know that what we do fits into the bigger picture of life. We need to know that what we do makes sense to others. And it is toward the Church with its many forms of recognition expressed in the liturgy and communal life that we look for some gesture of acknowledgment.

Here the Church can be both imaginative and creative. It can design liturgical gestures of recognition and blend them into a Eucharistic celebration. The Church might create a special rite for anointing family ministers. Special symbols, blessings or consecrations could be designed with reverence and meaning. What the Church would be saying is simple, yet utterly significant to those who receive its recognition: you ministers are important to the Church as it continues the mission of the Lord each day. Your efforts are deeply worthwhile. Your generosity and care merit our taking time to care for *you*! We do it now and we do it often: never should you go unnoticed or feel unappreciated.

Secondly, family ministers need guidance. Of course, much of that guidance will come from their interaction with one another. So ample time should be set aside for mutual discussion and consultation. These times together are important for developing a sense of shared ministry. Ministers need the opportunity to share both their worries and their dreams. Their perspective on particular issues is also sharpened in dialogue with others who confront similar situations.

Guidance might also take the form of formal training. Skills in leadership, communication and management provide both self-confidence and direction. Since one's efforts in ministry are done in the context of the life of the Church, guidance is also necessary from theology, particularly in the theological discussion of Church, sacrament, ministry, marriage and the family. These areas are experiencing some creative developments in theological thought, and constant updating of the family ministers is essential. A token presentation, a workshop or two, even a single course should never be considered adequate. Of course, the old principle of realism will enter because often the limitations of time, resources and personnel will demand their own concessions. Nevertheless, the ideal of continuing education should always be upheld. Again, creativity can be used to provide updating and direction. Experts can be brought to the local situation by audio or video means. And every community should be constantly alert for local persons who are often overlooked simply because they are local.

Skills in family ministry need not be viewed as esoteric or highly sophisticated. It is a form of ministry that looks toward common sense and practicality, and touches as closely as any other form the basic art of living and relating. It is a like-to-like ministry. These skills are rarely a matter of classroom instruction. We have to be reminded of this, given the emphasis on training in so many professions. This is not an argument against formal training as such. The point here is simply to call attention to the special case of family ministry as covering some very common areas of human and Christian life. Many can assist others, and themselves for that matter, without degrees or certified credentials. With practical and sound formal guidance, of course, they can be expected to do even more. What is needed most is an awareness of the God-given resources for ministry already present.

A third need of family ministers is enrichment. This can cover a multitude of areas, but here the emphasis is on their own spiritual enrichment. This is based on the simple axiom: the more we have, the more we will be able to give. Any minister in the Church is an ambassador of the Lord and will allow his or her own words also to be a carrier of the message of God. They permit their lives to speak of deep faith, confident hope and sensitive love.

These dispositions do not develop in a day. They call for nurturing and reinforcement. The ministers must have a healthy concern for their own Christian well-being. This is out of respect for the God who cares so deeply for them and for persons they are invited to serve in family life. It is also based on the value of caring for oneself. Christianity does not accept self-destruction for others. Here we are touching on an area of immense theological complexity, but the sacrifice in the Christian sense is more related to the root-meaning of that term, to make holy, than it is to the idea of destruction.

While ordained clergy and the professed religious consistently held personal holiness and its pursuit through a vital spirituality in the highest regard, the laity usually approached spirituality as a fringe area of concern. As the Church moves toward a deeper appreciation of the ministerial role of the laity, there will also have to be an accompanying value given to the spiritual development of the laity, particularly those involved in the specific ministries. Enrichment programs can be designed to correspond to the lifestyle and schedules of the laity. Programs can also be developed to support the spiritual development of the entire family. In summary, they should invite one to a deeper involvement in the Church and in ministry, as well as toward a more engaged participation in one's own family life.

A final need of family ministers is that of support. This will be quite similar to the recognition mentioned already, but it operates over the longer haul. Many of the family ministers of the Church will be volunteers. Time is a more precious commodity today. We'll give people almost anything before we give them our time. This is particularly due to the economic stresses today that often compel all the adults of the family to seek employment outside the home. Work schedules often cut into the precious free time of the weekend. What this means is that those who do give of themselves to family ministry will often be giving much through their commitment.

It also means that when their ministerial experience causes them occasionally to doubt their effectiveness, they will be more prone to give up. They will need a word of encouragement. Is this asking too much? Given our tendency to find fault with each other, to see the beam in each other's eye, it very well might be a major task for us to consider. It is difficult to explain the all-too-common situation where we fail to acknowledge each other's successes or where we fail to take time to sympathize with each other's difficulties. Of the four needs of leadership in family-life ministry, support demands the least allocation of funds, resources or time, but it may prove to be the most important—and the most forgotten. Let us pray that it isn't.

The Church's renewed concern for families covers many areas of family life as is evidenced in the six areas of ministry in the plan. It all begins, however, with family life *within* the family, and it is toward that setting that we now turn.

Chapter Six

FAMILY MINISTRY TOWARD THE INSIDE

W<small>E ARE ALL FAMILIAR WITH</small> the biblical warning: there is no real profit if you gain the whole world but lose your soul. This caution is not against "gaining" as such, but against a wrong set of priorities. It reminds us that our listing of preferences can be horribly out of line. This can happen simply because we don't take into account all that we should. We leave some significant areas outside the confines of our vision. Or it can

71

happen because, deep down, we know that if we set up our priorities in a certain way, it will be very hard to meet their demands.

This can often happen in reflecting upon the hard saying of Jesus: love your neighbor. The problem is to recognize the "neighbor" in the charge. Clearly, the title covers those in our neighborhoods, communities, nation and the world itself. And there is also the issue of their need for our recognition, affirmation and help. Neighborly love is conditioned not only by the person, but also by need because authentic love will be love expressed. It will be our response to their expressed need as well as their need for us simply to be a human being. That latter need is one that we all mutually share.

Yet there remains a context for neighbor love that is so close to us that it may be completely overlooked. It is the need to love the persons in our own families. The expression of that love will be the first form of family ministry.

It should be clear by now that when we discuss family ministry, our appreciation of "ministry" is person-centered and life-centered. This demands explicit mention, given the fact that our standard views of ministry have been closely bound to institutional or liturgical meanings. Even the concept "lay ministry" was often thought to be something that was properly done by the clergy, but owing to their insufficient numbers, the slack had to be taken up by lay persons. This was a common pattern in missionary situations.

Today we are moving to a more expanded notion of Christian ministry. The major shift concerns our appreciation of the *content* of ministry. That content rises from the center of our Christian life because it is directly related to our *life together*. Ministry serves to bring us to a deeper experience of each other, allowing us to enter more intensely and lovingly into the common human and Christian life we share. Ministry is aimed at overcoming the barriers, both personal and societal, which restrict communal life. Ministry is based on the conviction that our life together is of supreme importance to God; it is a unique reflection of God's own intense care and concern for us.

Once ministry is appreciated as touching communal life, it becomes applicable to the common, immediate, everyday events of life. It takes on concrete and inescapable meaning. It becomes a very personal part of the life of each Christian. And when we raise the issue of family ministry, the emphasis will fall directly on the communal life of one's own family.

To look with clear eyes at one's own marriage and family often takes no small amount of raw courage. It demands out-and-out heroism if we haven't looked for a long time. We all know that we are quite creative in fashioning imaginative portraits of how things are going. When asked, like Pavlov's famous pets, we reflexively respond: just great. And we hope the questioner won't pursue it any further.

This discussion of ministry within the family will be divided into its two common, although not universal, parts: ministry to one's marriage partner and the ministry to one's children. Recall that these are authentic Church ministries, since they are expressions of care and service within the domestic Church, the Church of the home.

Ministry to one's husband or wife has a range and depth difficult to circumscribe in any brief description. Marriage is community, but it is a particular type of community. In the shorthand of Vatican II, it is described simply as a community of love. Here is what the Council put forth as a Christian description of marriage:

The intimate partnership of married life and life has been established by the Creator and qualified by His laws. It is rooted in the conjugal covenant of irrevocable personal consent. Hence, by the human act whereby spouses mutually bestow and accept each other, a relationship arises which by divine will and in the eyes of society too, is a lasting one.[1]

The key idea in this description is the special covenant established in Christian marriage. It is founded both on the will of

[1]Pastoral Constitution on the Church in the Modern World, section 48.

God and the generous, loving wills of the marriage partners. The Council's words are an amplification of the biblical words: "What God has joined together . . . " The marital relationship is not simply another type of relationship or one possible way of establishing friendship. In the Christian context it is a very particular type of relationship. To gain a sense of its uniqueness, we shall examine some of the implications of this special type of relationship under its meaning for family, or here, spousal ministry.

Let us move right to the heart of the matter. "What God has joined together" proclaims that God is actually involved in marital life. God joins the couple as the wife and husband come together themselves. It is of vital importance not to separate the act of God from that of the couple. One way of grasping this mysterious joining is to conceive of God not as a presence outside the actual marriage relationship, but as a directing presence and energy within. God does not act above or below the lives of people he cares for. God acts *in* their lives. God draws the couple to each other and to himself as they freely move closer to each other. He is a guest within their relationship. He is part of their relationship, their love.

This acceptance of God's joining ought not to be interpreted as God using some kind of supernatural cement that cannot ever be separated by human force. God doesn't deal with us as if we were things. We were created as free persons, which also means that we bear responsibility for both our successes and failures. Yes, God can and does support our efforts. God acts for us and with us, but not in spite of us.

The reason for insisting on this cooperative image of Christian marriage is to show the need for marriage partners actively to develop their relationship. And this work (there is no better word) is their ministry to each other. If their relationship deteriorates, as it will if it is simply left untended, fault is to be found in their lack of positive effort. Of course, each marital relation will have its own story to tell. Each marriage will be somewhat unique because it is the joining of two quite singular persons, each bringing to the marriage an unprecedented personal history. We must always be on guard against appropriating images of so-called perfect marriages. Like the personal uniqueness invested in each of us at the moment of our creation by God, so also each marriage will have its own special character. What all Christian marriages must share, however, is a fundamental orientation of love, care and concern. Each marriage partner is charged with the responsibility of being *for* the other in a generosity that lives through the exciting moments of prosperity and good times, as well as through the flat and tepid moments of routine and poverty.

Also worth consideration is the fact that God's joining is not a one-time event, but a consistent activity corresponding to the *living* character of marital life. Just as a given couple will pass through various stages of marital crisis, and hopefully grow through the passages, so also does God become an ever more vibrant presence. Marriage partners will tell of ways that they come to reaffirm their marital promises. Each gains new insights into the marriage partner and into himself or herself, which occasion another look at their relationship. This new understanding calls forth a new commitment, and they remarry each other. This is not double-talk, but a meaningful way of describing the common processes of marital growth. As the years pass, new facets of personal identity surface, inviting a deeper level of acceptance and care. These deeper waters of apprehension prompt the couple to ask themselves whether they want to invest more. This invitation will appear risky, and some will shy away from this opportunity for greater intimacy, retreating into a more comfortable, more secure and less threatening posture. Those who continue the journey toward ever deeper levels of intimacy will know that authentic love is far different from what parades as love in our pop culture. In truth, the great lovers of our time will almost always be marked by years of experience, having confronted often the stresses of honestly living the shared life.

God has joined and is joining two very fragile and vulnerable human beings—a woman who appreciates herself enough to share her deepest secrets, dreams, fears and hopes—and a man who will do the same. Christian marriage is two persons who put themselves ''on the line'' for each other. This joining of themselves and their lives, coupled with God's supportive joining, creates a new love unit on the face of the earth, which becomes one of the great wonders of the world.

It should also be added that God's participation within marriage need not be construed as an extrinsic presence, an infringement upon our freedom or an encasement into slavery. God created us for our full development, and all divine direction and inspiration is toward our maximum perfection. Sometimes freedom within marriage implies that the wife and husband are allowed to do their own thing—privately and individually. The Christian vision of marriage is that of doing *God's* thing, and if this is grasped correctly, it results in being also what is absolutely best for the marriage partners. Marital development is toward an ever deeper experience of life and of life together.

Within the marriage relationship there ought also to be a deep mutual respect between the partners. This respect serves to protect the uniqueness of the person. It is the opposite of manipulation, where one person merely uses the other for his or her own self-centered purposes. This respect allows for a very special kind of freedom: the freedom to be who you are. Marital acceptance is an unreserved assent to the particularities and peculiaries of the other, who is accepted and loved most genuinely because the real other is involved. This kind of love has no need for pretense or disguise. It is a love that can be relaxed.

The establishing of Christian marital love demands both patience and endurance. The form and depth of its realization will always be conditioned upon the inherent, God-empowered capacities of the two incomparable persons who find themselves wife and husband. They are to be accepting of each other and yielding to the capacities of their particular relationship. This acceptance will often be the realization of the Christian virtue of reconciliation.

A spelling out of the dynamics of reconciliation in marital life will do much to concretize the meaning of ministry for marriage partners. This is largely due to the kind of expectations that persons bring into marriage, and because of the kind of descriptions popularly given to love in contemporary society. The expectations and hopes for marital life are often conditioned by the many widespread myths of love, from the catchy verses on greeting cards to the lyrics of popular songs. In rough form these myths speak of a special kind of relationship founded on romantic love. That love is "fallen into" as its influence is quite overpowering. When the person finds the one who was preordained as his or her "perfect" match, then it's simply a matter of psychological chemistry doing its thing.

What breaks down this myth is simply time, experience and the rise of inevitable conflict between the lovers. The couple begins to learn that interpersonal intimacy is a human achievement colored by all the ordinary assets and liabilities of the human condition. The task of loving another, who now appears as someone different from previous judgments, becomes as arduous an undertaking as anything imaginable. It calls upon our best abilities to understand and accept and adjust. Christian marriage comes to be a "hothouse" in which the whole composite of personal virtues and vices are brought into action.

When tension occurs and hurts take place the issue becomes: how is this to be resolved? First, there is the need to admit honestly that some conflict or variance has surfaced in the marital relationship. Then the couple will begin the process of building on some new foundations with additional material that was not envisaged in the original planning process. And they will have to forgive both themselves and each other for their previous narrowness. One of the most telling expressions of marital love will be this act of forgiving and the act of accepting forgiveness. It will be a special expression of God's forgiving love *in* the human fabric of relationship. Marital love will mirror not only the deep love of God, but also its forgiving side. Forgive us as we forgive each other.

There are many dimensions of Christian marital love that call forth the taxing exigencies of the Christian life. Here, we are simply reminded that these expressions are real statements of ministry. These expressions assist the couple in the achievement of an ever-deepening union of two quite different persons. Forgiveness and reconciliation are resources needed to deal with human self-centeredness in its many forms as it intrudes into the developing love-covenant between the couple. Reconciliation speaks not only of forgiving the past, but also of rejoining in a more complete relationship for the future.

Jesus often referred in parables to the hidden nature of the Kingdom of God. Was not part of his vision a sense that many of the really great events of the Kingdom of God on earth would be hidden from the eyes of the world? Was it not because these events would be the simple expressions of generosity, unadorned kindness and unpretentious generosity that occur daily in Christian marital and family life? This should be shouted from the housetops so that the tremendous significance of these common, yet so exhausting, acts allows them to receive the acknowledgment they deserve.

The potential areas of ministry between wife and husband are as extensive as is their daily interaction. The concerns of ministry will enter their life of communication, sexuality, and mutual support so necessary in a society that treats us more as functions than persons. The communal life of wife and husband touches most of the areas of ministry in the bishops' plan. The marital relationship cuts across "ministry for married couples," "ministry for developing families," "ministry for hurting families," and "ministry for parents." And the health and vitality of the wife-husband bond will be a major factor in the "results" of each of these areas.

The wife-husband relationship does not stand alone. While being a key factor in the life of the family, it will, with the exception of the childless marriage, be intricately bound into the life of parenting. And a clearly felt need in family life today is in the area of parenting. The task of "raising children" today is viewed as a major investment of both a personal and financial nature. This task becomes doubly difficult in the increasingly common situation of the single parent.

The plan for family life cites parenting as a special area of ministry. While the plan speaks of ministry *for* parents, it should also be mentioned that there is a ministry *of* parents. Repeating an earlier principle, it is important that this ministry be named. A parent in today's rather impersonal world gets precious little in the way of support for effort expended, often at great cost. In fact, what commonly occurs is not only a failure to thank the parent properly, for all that is done in assisting the development of the most precious "raw material" on the face of the earth, but the parent is also *blamed* for practically all the "sins" of the young. In a society where children experience the pervasive influence of the media and of their peers outside the home, somehow such influences are overlooked when the child exhibits some form of deviant behavior. Parents feel nonsupport from the wider society and from the many local communities that constitute their world. They often feel that the censure laid at their doorstep is misplaced. Is it any wonder that parents are asking for help? Who, they ask, will notice and respect their daily efforts at parenting?

The bishops' plan asserts that the Church will notice and that the Church will support their efforts. This is no small claim given the fact that the Church itself often participated in the process of blaming parents for the failures of their children. While this blaming was probably done unintentionally, parents nevertheless were made to feel inadequate when their children began to question certain beliefs of the Church or refused to attend the liturgy of the Church. The parents so often asked: what did I do wrong? And rarely was this question softened by the sensitive word of the Church, which might have said simply: you are not responsible for that which you cannot manage. Certainly the adolescent moves very resolutely outside the "management" of the parents, as he or she should.

Perhaps one of the first results of "ministry for parents" will be a sensitive and informed discussion in the parish as to the *real* responsibilities of the parent, which will include a careful mapping of where their realistic management ends. Obviously, this charting is not easy, but it will serve to provide a clearer understanding of the role of Christian parents.

One of the most effective ways to accomplish this will be to facilitate a discussion *among* parents, particularly of diverse ages.

One can acquire credentials in parenting by passing through the experience itself. The insights acquired and the skills developed can be of great benefit to others who are just beginning the process. There are, of course, recognized skills in parenting that focus on attitudes and communication techniques that also merit consideration. One of the common problems faced by most parents is the fear that their experiences and their children are uniquely odd and that other families are "normal." This generates feelings of inadequacy, and rather than dealing with the issue head-on, a parent will retreat into passivity and worry. It can be very healing to come to a realization that one's experience of parenting is indeed common, and that other parents have gone through similar crises and lived to tell about it!

With greater awareness and stress being placed on the role of parents as religious educators, a new area of potential "blaming" comes on the scene. While this area of responsibility is often stressed to enhance the parents' sense of value and dignity, what often results is another nail in the guilt-coffin. This will certainly occur when there is little specification of what this area of responsibility means in concrete practice. While there may exist in the mind of the parish priest, or the local religious education coordinator, a rather defined concept of the parents' role, it cannot be presumed that this is understood with any clarity by the average parent. The problem is only heightened when words like "primary" and "first" are joined with the already ominous responsibility of being a "*religious* educator."

The Church must take seriously the principles of the plan when it speaks of awareness, caring, and ministering with regard to parenting. The Church must come across as sensitive to the demands of parenting and supportive of its practitioners.

The Christian parent, in fact, is charged with major responsibilities, but it is the *whole* Church that must assist in the accomplishment of those charges. The child will ordinarily hear the word of salvation through the words and the deeds of the parent. The foundations of an open and healthy personality will be established though the many interactions of parent with child. The child's image of God will have something of the parent in it, and as we sense more and more the interrelational importance of communal life with religious life, the place of parents in the construction of that life will appear more decisive. We are not likely to see a lessening in the appreciation of the significance of the role of parent, but what we should look forward to is more assistance given to the parent in the living out of that role.

Nor should we overlook the effect of parenting on the parents! Their human and religious wholeness will be partly conditioned by the manner in which they express this generative function of their humanity. Religious reflection on the significance of caring for another, especially when this caring involves so much of the parents' human and Christian resources, can be a significant conversation in the Church. The local parish community can be a place where this conversation will take place.

Beginning with the marital relation and moving toward the experience of parenting, we take a trajectory that is very important for Christian awareness. It marks a passage from the self to others, from a center toward the outer boundaries. To be a Christian is always to be a missionary. A first "mission" is that to one's marriage partner. A second stage is toward one's children. The mission must, however, be extended further to those outside the family. We now take that next step.

Chapter Seven

FAMILY MINISTRY REACHES OUT

INCLUDED IN THE "JOB DESCRIPTION" of a Christian is the necessity of being a minister of the Lord. To be a Christian is to extend the care and concern of God to others who have both a need and a right to experience God's love in their lives.

One day a lawyer came to Jesus in search of a description of all that was needed for an individual to be saved. Starting with the "basics" Jesus restated the most vital commandments of the Law: to love God without reservation and to love one's neighbor as much as oneself. Wanting more explicit directives, the lawyer pursued his questioning further. He ventured one of the most important questions ever asked: who is my neighbor? The response of Jesus is recorded in Luke's Gospel with clarity and pathos. Jesus told a story that began: "A man was going down from Jerusalem to Jericho . . . " (Luke 10:30).

The parable of the Good Samaritan has excited the religious imagination of Christians. It has also tested their claims of virtue. Of particular significance has been the power of this story to call into question our tendency to create rather narrow views of social responsibility. Why does this rather simple story carry such weight? It is because of the nature of the human relationships between the characters of the story. The Samaritan extended himself for the beaten stranger much beyond what might be expected either from local custom or religious obligation. The brute fact was that Jews and Samaritans did not mix. Not even the near-death situation of the beaten man alongside the road established a claim upon the Samaritan who was on his own journey. But Jesus pointed to a real claim that went beyond the customary or the accepted. He stated in story form that we are all of God's family and that we were all to care for one another. Excuses based on racial differences or religious divergences are to be overlooked when it is a matter of genuine human need.

In the context of family ministry the point has been argued that social obligation clearly includes the "neighbors" in one's own family. But it must be added that the range of social responsibility must be extended to encompass those outside one's family. In the words of the bishops' plan: families are summoned to "look for opportunities beyond the immediate family to minister to the needs of others, especially needy neighbors, relatives and parishioners. Christian charity and justice call them to go out to serve the physical and spiritual needs of others in the local community, the country and the world."

The trajectory of concern moves from the nearer neighbor to those more distant. But the edge of responsibility never grows dull. This is not new teaching in the Church. The papal encyclicals of the last century consistently upheld a view of social responsibility that was worldwide in scope. In fact, the efforts of Christians for the enrichment of human and religious life is as long-standing as the Lord's mandate to feed the hungry, clothe the naked and give hospitality to the stranger. Meeting in a synod in 1971, the bishops of the world issued a plea always to keep in mind the needs of the poor and the helpless. In clear, unequivocal language they said, "Acting on behalf of justice is now a constitutive dimension of the Gospel."

Beneath their statement is the contention that the credibility of the Gospel is tied to the values and the lifestyles of those who claim it as their truth. Believability is related to the effective witnessing of its transforming power. The bishops were formulating in principle what a six-year-old will say if asked to comment on a common parental injunction: don't do as I do; do as I say. The language of our day might speak of authenticity. Scripture called it the living of the Truth.

Why does this matter have to be brought to the attention of families? Why does the recent statement of the bishops of the United States, "To Do the Work of Justice," mention explicitly the need to awaken in families a social ministry proper to their situation?

Perhaps it is because "family responsibility" might be so interpreted as to include all that needs be said about social responsibility. "Family" might then be used as a cover-up for a failure to consider and act upon responsibilities that rise from the wider community. This cover may be present in statements like the following: I have my family to watch out for first. With inflation being what it is, I'll have to make sure we have enough for the future. After all, charity does begin at home. Besides, what can one person do? The problems of poverty, injustice, maldistribution of resources, world hunger, the arms race—these are not going to be solved by me. Maybe they can't be solved. Anyway, I have all I can do to make my payments on time. That's just the way it is. And so the line of argument goes.

These words deserve a hearing. They are often said from an attitude of real responsibility. The economic pressures on families in our post-industrial era are real. Of particular importance for families is the high cost of raising children to the point where they are economically self-sufficient. Facile dismissal of this perplexity deservingly often falls on deaf ears.

Nevertheless all Christian families are members of and have responsibilities toward the wider human family of society. Facing those responsibilities is difficult, but no more so than the difficulty faced by the Samaritan when he came upon the helpless Jew on the side of the road. The family too will ask: who is my neighbor?

There are many ways to bring the family to a wider view of its social responsibilities. From a purely pragmatic standpoint, it can be pointed out that the family does not exist as an island. Its own health depends partly on the vitality of the wider society. The influence of the outside world impinges on the family as soon as the television set is turned on. It enters through the many contacts with the neighborhood and the local community, with the economic, educational and cultural influences that color everyday family life. To work toward the betterment of these outside realities could be motivated simply by what might be termed enlightened self-interest.

Christians, however, must create a much better foundation from which to move toward an active improvement of the world outside the boundaries of the immediate family. Today we are witnessing the strengthening of that foundation because the views of our sisters and brothers everywhere are becoming clearer through both personal and technological contact. Our understanding of their needs and our effective ability to meet those needs is also more realistic. Of course, we will have to look in order to notice these matters.

Most of all, our Christian reasons for service to others are more manifest than perhaps at any previous time. One way to bring this out is to recall some basic points from contemporary theological resources. Let us begin with the question: what is our Christian understanding of God? What view of God, appreciated both as Creator and Redeemer, as Initiator and Sustainer, as the One who empowers us as well as the One toward whom our efforts are ultimately directed, do we share as Christians? Of course, lengthy treatises have been written to portray God, so here we can hope only to offer a sketch. But we do want to appropriate elements of the portrait that establish a strong and sufficient reason for an expansive view of social responsibility.

Basic in that view of God would be a description of God's incredible generosity on our behalf. God possesses abundant riches in all the deep senses of that notion, and those riches are shared extravagantly with us. We know of no limits to God's bounty. Added to the gift of life itself is that of God's friendship, a friendship like no other. Even our personal rejections of God meet a willingness on God's part to begin again. While we may waste those riches for a time, the Father is always waiting with arms open and with celebration waiting.

What is our response to this state of affairs? It can be seen by joining the parables of the Prodigal Son with that of the Good Samaritan. The first parable speaks of wastefulness and forgiveness. It speaks of the son's sense of justice by returning with the hope of being treated only like a hired hand, and the father's magnanimous welcome back into the family. It is a story whose intent is to break open our sense of fairness and rightness. We are pushed to wonder about this strange world where loss is treated as if it were gain. We are tempted to complain with the son who remained at home: What's coming off here? This doesn't make sense.

What kind of response might we expect of the honored guest at the banquet? What is his feeling as he looks across the table at his father whose earlier gifts he had squandered in fast living and shallow pleasures? Can it be other than deep gratitude? Can it be other than a sense that he is living in a milieu of undeserved care and concern? And what might be his resolve if not to try to live that way himself?

What would be his response if he happened along on that road from Jerusalem to Jericho? Would he have passed the battered man in the ditch? Or would he have stopped to help. Might not he have recalled a feeling he once had of being battered and beaten, not so much by clubs or fists, but by the guilt of self-betrayal and by the thought of his filial defection?

Without doubt his personal appreciation of the gift of forgiveness would set him on a life's journey of generosity. And his calculations would not ask how little can I get away with, but how much can I give.

Who really is that "son" if not ourselves? Each one of us has been born to be in God's family and each one of us has at some time rejected and squandered his or her inherited riches. But we have been "re-gifted" by God's merciful love. We have retained our stature in God's family. This sets us on a course of gratefulness. Our life is not something to hoard for our private use. Rather we should be distinguished by generosity. We are empowered to express God's generosity to others. This reaching out to others in their need is a fundamental bearing of Church life. In the words of the Dogmatic Constitution on the Church of Vatican II, the Church is created to be a sacrament of God's presence in the world.

Sacrament means to embody in earthly form the effective attitude of God to others. The Church becomes the hands of God, doing the work of God. From stones of flesh and blood the Church fashions the Kingdom of God on earth. This earthly mission is of deep spiritual and human significance. And the Church's response to the mandate of "sacramentalizing" God in human form is crucial. God could have by-passed human means to create the New Creation, but instead God went the route of risk. In some way God took a chance with humankind by creating us with the gift of freedom. At times we have misused this gift either by failing even to act as free persons by allowing ourselves to be simply "of the masses" or by stopping short of the great expectations vested in us by God's intent. A clear delineation of these matters transcends our finite capacity to make precise judgments, but we can say that the gift of freedom carries with it a responsibility to respond, and for the Christian this includes the personal response of generously ministering to the needs of our many neighbors.

We sometimes pull back from this vision. We sense that we

might well lose something of our private selves, our more secure routines and securities, and our more comfortable lifestyles. We find ourselves wondering whether there might be some collateral that can be banked in safe places should all this not work out. We sense, like Pascal, that this Christian business involves a wager. Are we totally sure that we will not be burned by Christian altruism? But then we also come to recognize that it is only the child who demands certainty because of his or her worry over whether reality is capricious or irresolute. The child's world is still inhabited by goblins, monsters and other nefarious spirits bent on getting him as soon as he is not looking. So the child must ask the parent: Is it OK to go out? Will I be hurt?

The adult Christian accepts the world as tipped toward the good. God has a bias and it is for our best good. And the bias of God is particularly toward the poor and needy and the broken, and it is that bias that must be particularly evident in the life of Christians. Because of God's concern for the poor, the Christian family is to search out the helpless and be "good Samaritans."

Christian generosity is a matter of open-handed deeds. Let us therefore discuss what it might mean for the Christian family to live for peace and justice for the whole world and for the many little worlds that make it up.

First, within the family there ought to generate an appreciation of solidarity with all people. Parents will watch their language so as not to give the impression that some people are inherently of less value than others. This in itself is no small suggestion, given the widespread societal use of derogatory descriptions of racial, ethnic or national groups who are different. To have available in the home books and magazines describing the cultural and scientific achievements of diverse types of people is also worthwhile. Needless to say the Christian home should also be open to receiving guests without restrictions based on race, religion, ethnic background or social class.

Besides awareness of solidarity, the Christian family can concretize the value it places on service by sharing its resources and its time with those of less means. While this may often take the form of contributions of money or goods to persons unknown, the family should not overlook the opportunities for more direct assistance. Such help can be particularly possible at the neighborhood or parish level. One example is the recognition of the many needs of the elderly. Quite common is the situation where older citizens are living alone, often cut off from family. It is also difficult for many to request help from neighbors. Sometimes their own pride is involved. Sometimes they are simply shy. Whatever the case, the Christian family that is sensitive to its responsibilities for others will find ways to help that respect the dignity of these neighbors or parish members.

One of the most salient characteristics of family ministry is its interpersonal emphasis, and one of the most common, yet hurtful, experiences of modern life is that of loneliness. Perhaps one of the basic goals of family ministry, then, could be the going out to the lonely, the shut-ins and the shut-outs of society. One form of genuine family ministry over the years has been that of foster-parenting. It flows from the heart of family life: the nurturing capacity of caring parents in accepting children. The care of foster children may be one of the great, yet unacknowledged, areas of exceptional virtue present today. Family ministry will also take the form of helping other couples or families. Unfortunately, we have grown so accustomed to the myth of self-sufficiency that we think neither of helping nor of seeking help from other families. What results is that many families hurt in solitude and silence.

Somehow we will have to grow out of this myth toward a wholesome acceptance of the reality of interdependence. Formerly, interdependence was more or less forced on people. People had to pool their resources because there weren't enough to go around. Every family didn't possess a complete array of tools. Many projects depended on the combined effort of the neighborhood, and people felt free enough to ask for assistance. With the rise of a "do-it-yourself" culture, people are made to feel inadequate if they have to ask for a helping hand.

What is even more difficult is to ask for help in matters having to do with life's inevitable trials. We may more easily ask the advice of Ann Landers than that of a neighbor or relative. But isn't the task of living meant to be a shared venture? Are we not intended to shoulder one another's burdens from time to time?

A blueprint of how each family ought to reach out to others cannot be drawn. What your family does in the way of meeting the needs of others will depend on your own resources. It will also depend somewhat on the strength of your own family life. The "somewhat" was included intentionally because, first, no one ever gets it *all* together, so to speak; and second, because in the very act of reaching out, a family is strengthened. Further, the specific shape of our service to others will depend on our own awareness of what others realistically need and what we can realistically provide. Ministering to others is not simply an exercise in doing good. It must be based on a sound judgment of the best interests of others, not what we imagine their needs to be. Part of the responsibility of service is the "research" that goes into the discernment of real needs.

The "Plan of Pastoral Action for Family Ministry" is designed "to help families become aware of their special charisms, talents and potential for self-help and ministry to others." What comes to mind here is the challenge to the Church to facilitate meaningfully the expression of the latent generosity of Christian families. What do parishes do with imagination and realism to raise the awareness of their communities to the social issues within their own ranks and those outside their boundaries? Does the local Christian community meaningfully care even for the needs that are certainly present among its own? There are some religious sects in this country that are exempt from the Federal Government's social-security program. Some religious groups reject the need for life insurance. Do these people have any need for security? They do, but their security is based on their confidence in the generosity of their neighbors within their religious community. If death, illness or other forms of personal tragedy happen, the community spontaneously responds with whatever assistance is needed.

Is there the same kind of generosity present in the religious community of Roman Catholics? This is not an argument to follow the way of those who reject the benefits of social security or life insurance. But it does raise a serious question as to the sense of social responsibility present in the community. Do we *really* care about each other? Do we care about the family life of our neighbors? Are we bothered by the inequitable distribution of the world's wealth? Does our effective concern for others move beyond the enclosure of our own family?

The bishops' plan is *for* family life. But there is a hard edge inherent in that concern because it is inviting families to assume genuine leadership in the area of social ministry. The plan emphasizes that we are have "charisms, talents, and potential for self-help and ministry to others." Let us begin a conversation as to what these abiding gifts might be. Without neglecting the real responsibilities to our own families, let us open our hearts, our homes and our families to the outside. A house can become pretty stuffy if the doors and windows are not opened occasionally to let the fresh air blow through the rooms. So also with us. We can become rather stale Christians.

The early Church seemed to have a good sense of this outgoing dimension of family ministry. One of the most common questions raised, when a judgment was made as to the authenticity of the Christian life of the community, was this: Do they care for the widows and the orphans? These were the family people without the common supports of family life. Who was to care for them if not other families?

Along this same line, Vatican II in its Decree on the Apostolate of the Laity expressed the following: The Christian family should concern itself with "the adoption of abandoned infants, hospitality to strangers, assistance in the operation of schools, helpful advice and material assistance for adolescents, help to engaged couples in preparing themselves better for marriage, catechetical work, support for married couples and families involved in material and moral crises, help for the aged not only by providing them with the necessities of life but also by obtaining for them a fair share of the benefits of an expanding economy" (section 11).

The range of the Council's concern was broad indeed, but it had to be in order to encompass the realistic parameters of our common Christian responsibility. Note that there is also mention of efforts toward the improvement of society in terms of its delivery of benefits and services to those most in need. National and local laws and policies are not made in heaven. They are forged in our legislatures and executive offices by our elected representatives. Part of our Christian responsibility is to watch over governmental action, especially where there might be inequity or where the needs of the helpless are overlooked.

The same Council document on the laity says that Christians are "to make sure that governments give due attention to the needs of the family regarding housing, the education of children, working conditions, social security, and taxes; and that in policy decisions affecting migrants their right to live together as a family should be safeguarded" (section 11).

What comes across in this discussion of family ministry is that whatever is done, with each family setting its own agenda, it should be something quite concrete. It is satisfying to hang inspiring banners and stirring plaques on the walls of our homes. A family that prays together is doing something most worthwhile. But there ought also to be in the family a wholesome and receptive sense of the outsider, i.e., those who do not belong to the immediate family but who do belong, with us, to the larger family of God.

Chapter Eight

FAMILY LIFE AND EVANGELIZATION

THE FIRST CHRISTIANS WERE all missionaries. After witnessing the risen Jesus and experiencing the Spirit in Jerusalem, the first Christians hit the road. They were responding with their feet to the parting words of Jesus: "Go therefore and make disciples of all nations . . . " (Matthew 28: 19). They were sent to tell about all that they had heard and saw. They were even reminded to mention what they had eaten. Everyone was to be let in on the Good News: We are all loved by God—repent—turn your heart—and live as favored members of God's family!

93

The spirit of that community was one of zestful enthusiasm for what they were to communicate. There were, of course, hard times with the constant threat of persecution and, one would have to add, the world wasn't exactly ready to receive with open arms those ragamuffins from the backhills of Galilee. But these pioneers of the Gospel persisted, and when we Christians tell the story of our roots, we are proud to include in that telling stories about Peter and Paul and Timothy.

We are now separated by almost 2,000 years from those days of dawn, yet by divine mandate we stand under the same charge: "Go therefore and make disciples of all nations . . . " We must be reminded of this side of our Christian life because of a tendency to become overly concerned about other things. During the pontificate of Paul VI the Catholic Church experienced a history that was perhaps unparalleled in terms of rapid change in almost every facet of Church life. There is little evidence that the pace of change will subside even now, given the fact that the Church has clearly decided to remain immersed in the dynamics of cultural change to insure that the incarnational dimension of Christianity comes through. Squarely in the midst of post-Vatican II Church life, Paul VI in 1975 produced what was called "an apostolic exhortation" of extreme importance entitled "On Evangelization in the Modern World" (*Evangelii Nuntiandi*). It flowed from the Pope's deep pastoral concern over the spiritual condition of contemporary life, and out of a desire to insure that the Church reforms of Vatican II took place within the authentic spirit of the Christian Gospel. The exhortation was a reminder to keep first things first, and above all, not to forget our roots.

Paul VI asserted that the emphasis on evangelization was not some new tactic in Church life nor an element inherent in some recent theological fad. Rather it arose from the heart of the Council's fundamental intent "to make the Church of the twentieth century ever better fitted for proclaiming the Gospel to the people of the twentieth century" (*E.N.*, 2). Evangelization, he argued, comes also from the heart of genuine Church life. With simplicity and strength the Pope affirmed that the Church "exists in order to evangelize" (*E.N.*, 14). It would hardly be necessary to remind an earlier Paul about this as he stepped from the boat at the

Mediterranean port of Corinth. Yet it may be very important that this be made known in the corridors of the Vatican, in the halls of the United States Catholic Conference in Washington, D.C., in the churches of Chicago, Illinois, and Yakima, Washington. And it may also be worthwhile to let something of this take shape over the breakfast table of Christian families.

Some new facts have been used to describe the present condition of the Church in the United States. We now hear discussions about the "unchurched" who are not touched by any kind of Church life. They number about 20 percent of the population. These are people who do not consider themselves a member of any particular Church and who do not attend church services. We also hear about the 6.6 million baptized Catholic children of school age (1976 figures) who are not enrolled in any formal religious-education program. It is estimated by the National Opinion Research Center in Chicago that about 15 percent of those who were raised Catholics no longer consider themselves within the fold of that community.[1]

With these "realities" in mind the Catholic Church of the United States has pledged an all-out effort to take the posture of evangelization as it moves into the dusk days of the twentieth century. No one can be critical of this priority. If the Catholic Church is to be a genuine Church of the Lord, it must proclaim the Good News both in good and in hard times.

The issue becomes difficult when talk must turn to deed and the community must sit down to decide what this evangelization effort means for the day-to-day life of the Church. This conversation has begun and it has taken some very significant turns, especially with regard to family life. The bishops of the United States now see that the effort of evangelization must be directly coordinated with two other salient pastoral priorities: the renewal of the local parish and the development of family-life ministry.

While it remains to be seen how the interrelation of these efforts will be enfleshed in Church life, it must be admitted that

---

[1]Andrew Greeley, *Crisis in the Church*. Chicago: Thomas More Press, 1979, p. 15.

there is notable wisdom in the correlation of these pastoral objectives. Here is why. For the vast majority of Catholics parish and family represent the contexts for both the genesis and the living out of their Christian and Catholic life. Furthermore, these two contexts ought to be taken together as well, because in the existential order the effects of each communal body will spill over into the other. Looking back into the history of the Catholic Church in the United States, there did not seem to have been an overt plan to establish parish and family as the key religious contexts, but it has come about.

From a theological standpoint this might be explained in the following way. Deeply present in the Christian view of life is an abiding claim that authentic religion and genuine community go hand in hand. Earlier we recalled Paul's entry into Corinth. What did he do once he gained a hearing for his message? Did he not advise those who accepted the Word to form a community? After his departure, was not that community the new custodian of the Word? And has that not been the pattern of spreading the Word ever since?

All of us begin our sojourn on earth in a community. Our human development arises from our participation in community. Our deeper feelings of satisfaction or failure will usually be tied to the community that we satisfied or failed. Clearly there is a personal side to life, but it is inseparable from a communal side. If this is true from a purely human standpoint, will it not also ring true from a religious standpoint?

With regard to our Christian appreciation of parish and family life, we have already noted some significant advances registered at Vatican II in terms of pointing to the authentic ecclesial status of both parish and family (see Chapter Three). Part of the reason for naming these communities as real expressions of Church was what might be termed a *de facto* argument. In actuality the context where the Word of salvation is first heard, first reponded to, first celebrated and first lived is *in* these communities. In sacramental terminology the presence of the Spirit is at work *in* the relationships that constitute those communities.

Therefore, when we speak of evangelization, we do well to finish the sentence with something about family and something about parish.

The relation between family life and parish renewal will be treated in the next chapter. Here we want to explicate the connection between evangelization and family life. A first question might be: Did Paul VI note any connection in his apostolic exhortation? Here are his own words:

One cannot fail to stress the evangelizing action of the family in the evangelizing apostolate of the laity. At different moments in the Church's history and also in the Second Vatican Council, the family has well deserved the beautiful name of "domestic Church." This means that there should be found in every Christian family the various aspects of the entire Church. Furthermore, the family, like the Church, ought to be a place where the Gospel is transmitted and from which the Gospel radiates. (Section 71.)

The Pope notes two basic expressions of the evangelizing potential of the family. The first is within the family itself. There we may speak about the Gospel as it is expressed between the marriage partners and between the parents and their children. A second dimension concerns the communication of the Gospel from the family to outsiders. Given the creative dynamic of life within the family toward life outside the family, as was described in the last two chapters, it is worth mentioning that a similar dynamic is operative in the context of evangelization. Both contexts should be appreciated *and interrelated* in forming specific pastoral strategies for evangelization.

Within the family there should be what might be called an evangelical undercurrent to the relational life. Here care must be taken to understand just what is meant by taking that approach. The problem is that the term "evangelical" has been used quite extensively in the history of our country, although admittedly its use in the Catholic Church has been infrequent. Often "evangelical" referred to a particular method of preaching or to a specific style of Church life. It was often associated with a fundamentalistic approach to the Bible.

When we speak of an evangelical undercurrent, we mean that the common activities and expressions of family life ought to be expressed in harmony with the basic Christian orientation found in the Gospel. To be evangelical is to be Christian. It also means that the Christian side of things gains some explicit mention in the family. This can come about through some expression of family prayer (which has been a strong side of Catholic family life), through the common reading of Scripture, or through family rituals that carry a religious meaning as well. Most of all, the inherent quality of family relationships, the level at which they embody Christian care and concern, express the greatest degree of evangelical content. "By this all men will know that you are my disciples, if you have love for one another" (John 13:35).

The message of Good News is the word that we *can* live together in intimacy and trust and support. The Gospel is true because it can bring us to make sense out of this fragile life we have been given. The Gospel is true because we discover our deeper selves in the intimacy of acknowledgment and acceptance of one another. What we discover is that we are accepted in all our limitations, liabilities and yes, even in our sinfulness. We learn this not simply by reading it on the page of a book or in the fine words of a gifted preacher, but in the eyes and in the embrace of another human being. The Gospel becomes alive because we gain a deeper sense of life in the communal life of intimacy where our real self, the self behind the mask and role, comes out.

In the words of Paul VI: "In a family which is conscious of this mission, all the members evangelize and are evangelized" (*E. N.*, 71). Clearly whatever effort the Church makes toward the strengthening and enriching of family life will enhance the capacity of that family life to be more evangelical. Also hinted in the words of the Pope is an appreciation of a "systems theory" of family life. One cannot separate the one who "speaks" the Gospel from the one who "hears" its salvific message. Like family life itself this process is in continuous flux; even the word of the youngest child may at a given moment be *the word* for the family. It may a word of hope in the midst of a dark night or simply a contagious smile that dries some tears of frustration.

The task before us is to translate the more religious-sounding language of traditional theology and spirituality and the more "churchy" language of Scripture into the actual dynamics of family life. If this is done effectively, we will be able to expose for common view elements of our everyday life that have deep Christian significance. As we saw in our discussion of ministry, the mere naming of these realities does much to enhance their transforming power. Paul VI speaks of being *conscious* of the mission to evangelize. Part of that consciousness will be an *awareness* of the daily events of family life as they carry the saving word of the Gospel. The Christian family can then begin to understand why it is entitled to be called "Christian." It is invited to make present, and to make real, the personal love of God in the accepting, supporting and healing actions of their life together. In making these dispositions real, the family becomes "sacramental" in that it expresses in human gesture the real presence of God.

Who is to see these gestures? Are they to be simply for the "enjoyment" of the family within the walls of its own home? If they are part of the general dynamic of authentic Christianity, they will be for others as well. It will be quite difficult, if not impossible, to program what we can call the witness dimension of Christian family life, but we can discuss some of its possible effects.

Earlier in this book (Chapter Three) we discussed the Christian family's orientation toward the acceptance and nurturing of new life. What we found in the heart of the family was an out-going generosity rooted in the appreciation of God's generosity. Unalloyed love was seen to be creative of life. Within the family the exchange of personal knowledge and love on both a conscious and unconscious level contributes vitality to the persons involved. Personal life is sensed as dynamic and vibrant, capable of both intensification and diminution. Life can be either "more" or "less."

One way of interpreting the reason for the Incarnation of

Jesus is to explain his coming in order to make possible for us a greater entry into life. In his own life Jesus exemplified a style of relating to people and to events which offered evidence that this greater life was possible. We might describe that style in many ways. He was not afraid of challenges even if his own life was in the balance. He was receptive to every kind of person imaginable, in a society which placed stern limits on whom one should meet and on whom one should avoid. He was generous with the weak and fainthearted. He confronted the deceitful and the unscrupulous. He was particularly disturbed by those who used religion for personal gain. He was, above all, "a man for others."

Jesus' going out to others empowered them to live more fully. That same "power" has been entrusted to the Church and is made real whenever there is the same kind of "going out" that Jesus did. We call this "ministry" or Christian service. We discussed this at length in the last chapter and how this takes form in Christian family life. The point here is to affirm the *connection* between Christian ministry and the act of witnessing. The primary form of evangelization for the Christian family to those outside the family will be the preaching of the word of service. It will be a word encased in deed. Those who observe the outgoing care of the family will be prompted to ask: Why do they do what they do? What are their motives?

Should the family be directly asked, they should be ready to give an explanation for the hope that is in them. They can then tell the story of God's love for them and why they desire to share that love with others. This witnessing to God's bias toward us is a participation in the prophetic ministry of Jesus. The Dogmatic Constitution on the Church of the Second Vatican Council specifically mentions family life as a special expression of that ministry. While describing the apostolic mission of the laity, the Council declares: "For that very purpose He made them His witnesses and gave them understanding of the faith and the grace of speech, so that the power of the Gospel might shine forth in their daily social and family life" (*Lumen Gentium*, section 35).

Like the shape of family ministry adopted by a particular family, the shape of the family's evangelizing efforts will vary. A given couple or family may become involved in an explicitly religious form of ministry. They may give of themselves in helping others develop better marriages and families as is done in the Marriage Encounter movement. They may become teachers of religious education. They may embark on a ministry in nursing homes, a hospital or in a home for the elderly. They may, as a family, volunteer for the home or foreign missions. There are many ways the Christian family might express what the one Word of God utters: You are loved, so live generously.

To express that word with fidelity and perseverance the family needs the support of other families and like-minded persons. They need not only to hear again the saving Word of God, but they also need to come together to celebrate its presence and power. For this purpose the family also reaches out to join in a wider community of learning, service and celebration. That community will commonly be the parish, and the family will play a vital role in the effort to create authentic Christian community in that context. What follows speaks of families and the parish. It also speaks of the parish family.

Chapter Nine

FAMILY LIFE AND PARISH RENEWAL

ONE OF THE MOST OBVIOUS, yet probably unpredicted, results of Vatican II on parish life was the creation of a vast variety of parish styles and structures. It is so common to hear comments about that far-out church across town or that sleeping parish in the inner city that we hardly reflect on the novelty of these remarks. Before the Council the primary distinguishing features among parishes were factors like the personality of the pastor, whether the parish had summer sermons or the won-lost record of the parish grade-school basketball team. While these may still be important in some parishes, what usually distinguishes parish life today is something more fundamental and significant.

Without trying to escape into broad generalities, what seems to be most important in parish life today is its *vitality*. An irony of contemporary Church life is that we probably have a better theological and human understanding of parish than ever before, but that wealth of knowledge doesn't seem to get into the actual lifeblood of parishes. At the present time the *Official Catholic Directory* lists close to 18,600 parishes in the United States. In terms of Church life the parish remains at the heart of the action or inaction as the case may be. As Church renewal continues as the top priority since the Council, the bishops of the United States have adopted parish renewal as a basic context for achieving that goal.

How is parish life constituted these days? What are the building-blocks out of which this renewal is to be constructed? How is the post-Vatican II parish different from the parish of the 40's or 50's? These questions are necessary because parish renewal is a flesh-and-blood issue. The success of that renewal will not depend so much on fine plans established in a diocesan chancery office, but on the personal gifts and talents of those who *are* the parish, because a parish is basically made up of people.

One of the most apparent changes in the parish is the composition of the work-force of the parish. Before the Council the workers were primarily the pastor, his assistants, the parish secretary, the sisters who taught in the parochial school and the janitor. Their method of operation was simple: each did his or her own job. Except to get "work orders," their interrelationship was minimal. It was primarily a businesslike situation. Most would say that the parish ran fairly smoothly. What happened was reliable, predictable and fairly pleasant.

Then came the Council with its mandate for change. The first wave of changes were liturgical and some new "workers" were brought into the parish picture. They were called commentators. Part of their job assignment was to give directions on when the congregation was to sit or stand. They also delivered some of the readings. About the same time in another part of the parish another set of "workers" was being enlisted. These were the volunteer teachers of religious education. The laity had been brought into two significant areas of parish life: the liturgy and the religion class.

The Council further suggested that each parish create a parish council as an advisory committee to the pastor. In some parishes these councils were asked to make some very important decisions, such as whether or not to close the parochial school. Like the spirit of parishes mentioned earlier, councils varied considerably from parish to parish. In some parishes the pastor flatly refused to create a council.

What is going on beneath all these modifications is a matter of Church *ownership*. This is not meant in the formal economic sense, but in the personal sense. Who really owns the parish? What does it mean to *belong* to a parish community? What does all this talk about participation in Church life really mean? What does ministry in the Church mean? And further, what does shared ministry mean?

The Council gave a rather clear picture of what Church life meant when it described the Church as the People of God. As was mentioned in our earlier discussion of the various meanings of Church (see Chapter Three) this description was intended to communicate the *full* membership *in* the life of the Church for all. In that same context the Council went on to stress that each person possesses special gifts or charisms that are to be respected in Church life.

Some of this gradually is surfacing in parish life. Now the "work force" has expanded in many parishes to include religious and lay persons in positions of authentic pastoral responsibility. There is developing in some quarters the notion of corporate ministry, which is a sense of ministry that flows from the combined efforts of Christians who see their personal strengths enhanced by operating from a base of shared decision-making, communal prayer and discernment and mutual support. These pastoral teams are apt to be a rich composition of personalities or gifts and may signal a wave of the future in ecclesial management.

One of the basic tasks of parish renewal is the creation of a greater sense of Christian *community* in the parish. This charge can appear staggering given the size and diverse make-up of many parishes. If one evaluates the pre-existing natural communities within the typical parish boundaries, one can find even more cause for a pessimistic prediction as to the outcome of significant community-building at the parish level. The last census in the United States pointed out that the majority of Americans live in what is, in general, a suburban setting. Now our satellite bedroom communities do not have a reputation for creating outstanding communal ties. Most of them lack a focal point, a place for people to meet, greet and talk with other people. In fact, the main street of many locales in our country will be an interstate highway!

What can a parish do to fashion a sense of community? Is this a totally unrealistic goal given the natural distances that exist among us in a country which is sometimes called "a nation of strangers"? Might there be a clue to parish renewal in the renewed effort for family ministry? After all, parishes are made up not only of individuals but also of families. Is there perhaps an answer to this dilemma embedded in the fact that many parishes report their population as a certain number of *families*, and not by a head-count of individuals?

Before we delve further into the possible interface of family life and parish renewal, we should make some distinctions about community, as we know about it from the social sciences. Evelyn Eaton Whitehead makes a significant distinction in her own analysis of parish life by reminding us that sociologists speak of community sometimes in reference to primary group experience and sometimes simply as a social form.[1] The *experience* of community provides us with a sense of belonging, of sharing a common viewpoint or understanding, of being cared about as a person,

[1] *The Parish in Community and Ministry.* New York: Paulist Press, 1978, p. 37.

and of being in genuine communion with others. It seems that when we despair over forming community on the parish level, we are more or less thinking about the experience of the rather intense community described above.

The other way of construing community is to think about it as a social form. Here the emphasis is on facilitating the coming together of people, particularly to engage in a common task or project. Primary group experience may arise during the accomplishment of the task, but it is not of the essence of that kind of community. Mutual communication and interaction with a sense of commitment to the group goals and ideals are expected. Community in this sense has a stronger bonding power than does what might be called a formal institution or association. We might say that communality exists in a continuum, the extremes being intense primary-group experience at one end, and loose association or affiliation at the other. Parish community will lie somewhere in between.

With communality in a continuum we can also develop a sense that the parish may be moving either toward or away from a greater degree of community. This "mapping" of the process of community-building can bring the task into a more workable framework. The parish can ask itself whether it is moving toward greater communality or not. It can also lay down some realistic and creative plans even more effectively to accomplish that goal. And in beginning, with some concrete program, it is taking the most important step on the journey.

Might there be some short-cuts toward achieving a better level of community in the parish? What about the families? Has the Church really approached the issue of parish life from *their* perspective? What about parishes who claim to be pro-family because they have something for every member of the family? They have a mothers' club, a St. Vincent de Paul society, a C.Y.O. and youth soccer and volleyball program for youngsters. They also have religious education for *all* ages. There is the C.C.D. program for the grammar-school kids, a very active and exciting high-school program, and an adult religious-education series that is quite popular. There is even a pre-school religious ed program that meets at the same time as the parish Mass on Sunday.

Does this scenario appear familiar? Does this even sound like it might be a rather good parish? Or might there be a bug in the system that jeopardizes the whole effort? What is the meaning of family in the parish just sketched? The family provides the persons who participate in the programs. The family is a "feeder" community for the parish. Is this not the playing out of a common theme in parish life: ask not what the parish can do for the family, but what the family can do for the parish?

Let us return to the issue of community-building. While our neighborhoods or subdivisions may not be natural communities anymore, the family is! Is there not a way to plan parish life in such a way that families are allowed to remain intact as they participate in the ordinary affairs of the parish? Can we so design our liturgical life, our religious-education programs, our various expressions of ministry and outreach around the family? We may ask, does that not leave out the single people? This does not have to happen because of two types of strategies that may be employed. First, single persons are usually tied to some kind of family situation, if only a type where a group of friends forms a community of mutual support and friendship. The parish could work with these groups. Second, in a nonthreatening way, single persons could be invited to join with families in parish programs. This may be of particular benefit for elderly persons who are single and live alone. This, of course, should not be forced. The point is that the parish should think of its members as already *in* communal groups, and should build on the living communities already there.

This approach has the potential for revolutionizing ordinary parish activities. Take, for example, the parish liturgy and religious-education program. Some parishes already have a sense of this in programs that prepare young children for the reception of the sacraments of Penance and Eucharist. Some continue the spirit by having the children actually receive these sacraments with their family. Sensitive pastoral situations where, for example, there may be an interfaith marriage are usually handled well when the matter is discussed beforehand and adjustments are made to deal with these special cases.

Such programs are only a beginning to what could be. Every scientific survey of the effectiveness of religious education has pointed to the family as the crucial element. Nevertheless the common pattern in religious education is to exclude systematically the family from participation *as a family*. There are significant exceptions to this pattern, but they are exceptions. Dolores Curran, in a talk given to religious educators in Ohio in 1978, offered a challenge to parishes to suspend their ordinary pattern of religious education for one year. During that time, she said, deal *only* with family units. Gather family groups, provide educational resources for the home, in a word, declare a moratorium on educating the individual for a while and educate families.

If the parish redesigns its life around family life, parish life will lose some of its efficiency and neatness. It will become more like the life in an average family: a combination of order and chaos. More persons will certainly be brought into the act. Coordination of this effort may prove to be a monumental task, but we might recall that one of the most effective ways of forming community is to get people involved in a common task. If we follow the suggestion of Dolores Curran, what have we really got to lose? It's not as if we were closing down parish operations for a year. Is the suggestion threatening? Of course it is, because it is asking for the *radical* modification of a pattern that has been around for as long as most of us can remember. And if the parish decides on a less than total moratorium on traditional programs, it ought to at least assist parents more in their involvement in family catechesis, which Pope John Paul II stresses in his encyclical letter, *Redeemer of Man* (section 19).

From a theological standpoint what will result is one basic form of the Church interrelating and *respecting* another form: the local church serving the family, and the domestic church building up the parish. The image of "building up" is significant because the parish community will only be created out of the communities formed by the smaller groups within itself. This brings us to another promising approach to parish renewal that has developed most particularly out of the experience of the Church in Latin America. Our reference is to the rising number of grassroots, small religious communities called *comunidades de base*, or basic Christian communities.

These groups are generally small; they embody a high degree of solidarity and serve religious, social and sometimes economic functions. They have been particularly successful in the poorer rural areas of Latin America. Many have a strong evangelical purpose as in Paraguay, where they are called "servants of the Word."

The significance of the small religious group has been quite evident in the experience of the Church in the United States, but it was often not tied to a parish base. In fact, practically every spirited religious movement within the Church has had its type of small group structure. Does this say something about parish life? It should, and in many parishes there is a process going on to parcel the parish into smaller units. These "block units," as they are sometimes called, perform many functions. They may meet for shared prayer or liturgy. They may establish an educational or ministerial program for themselves. In short, they seek to encompass the basic functions of the parish, but do so in a more participatory way. It's difficult to find a back pew in a living room.

One of the problems of family life in contemporary society is the isolation felt by the individual nuclear family. Our living patterns have cut into some of the close ties that formerly kept the extended family at least in close proximity to itself. This is not to romanticize those good old days, but in times past there was at least a feeling that there were others around to whom you could go without apology and ask for help.

Can the parish do something to improve this situation? Can it not facilitate the coming together of people in small communities where the faith can be shared and lived a bit more consciously than is now the case? The family itself also needs these wider contexts to begin expressing its own need to go out to others in ministry. It appears on the surface at least to be a "no-lose" situation. And it will put the Church into the wider community in a promising way in that neighbors will be given an opportunity to share more than cocktails and gossip.

Families will then have the opportunity to share with other families something of their faith, the personal touch they bring to their religious life. There can also develop a mutual understanding that the members of these smaller groups can depend on one another for the kinds of things that in the past were expected from cousins or other close kin. In the apostolic Church there developed the custom of Christians approaching each other as "brothers and sisters in the Lord." What was operating was an extension of the family sense into the local Christian community. While this same attitude may be impossible even to imagine in a parish community, it may well be possible to engender it in a smaller community, or network of families.

These smaller communities are not intended in the least to bring about the dismantling of the local parish. Rather they are to function as living cell structures within the parish community. They will insure not only that the parish Eucharistic liturgy will serve to create community, but also that it will celebrate the existing communities which have been created by the Spirit—all through creative and realistic pastoral planning. As the Rite of Christian Initiation for Adults states, the parish is a community of communities.

Parish liturgies can also be occasions of celebrating family life in the belief that the Spirit is present and active in those religious communities as well. The Eucharist is a celebration of what has gone before, with particular focus on the death and resurrection of our brother and Lord, Jesus Christ. It is also a celebration of the present riches of the community gathered in common meal as they commit themselves as a body to a deeper expression of God's love in their lives. Finally, the Eucharist is a banquet of hope or, in traditional language, a pledge of future glory. We Christians need to hear words of hope because it is the power of hope that excites us to go beyond our narrow and hesitant views of what we are capable of doing. Like most people, we Christians tend to be underachievers, not because we don't have the strength, but because we don't believe enough in ourselves. If we are to be a people of hope, and if we are to have hope in Christian family life, we may need some new approaches. Our final chapter will suggest just that.

Chapter Ten

FAMILY LIFE AND ITS HOPEFUL FUTURE

A<small>T</small> THE CONCLUSION OF the second installment of *Roots*, Alex Haley appeared before the television camera to talk about the importance of family. One of the ways he suggested that we could capture a strong sense of family was to hold periodic family reunions. These planned reunions are necessary now, he indicated, because our extended families are often spread from coast to coast, and for some, even farther.

Sometimes these gatherings have their moments of awkwardness. For instance, there is the basic issue of who's who. The fact that the appearances of people change through the years needs no other proof than a casual look around. Both faces and physiques change with the latter usually receiving more comment. Generally, however, there is a good feeling, a feeling of history, and a feeling that we, as a family, are important and worth preserving.

Haley also recommended that some of the elders of the family be asked to recount their memories. In their telling, the history of the family would be made known, especially to the younger members. We know what the telling of Alex Haley's family history did for our entire national psyche. The power released in the telling of our own family story is a personal resource well worth capturing. Something of the very energy of life is contained in those memories.

Memories are very powerful ingredients of life. If they are good recollections, they exist not only in the past but continue on as assets in the present. They must, however, be known if their riches are to be mined. They must be put into the fund of the conscious life of the family.

To be personal for a moment, if I were asked: Suppose your house were on fire. After you were assured of the safety of your family, what next would you save? my answer would be, simply, the pictures of my family. Everything else in that house would be replaceable, but the memories stored in these pictures would not. Besides, the value of those pictures, in terms of their power to recapture events and moments of the *life* of my family, is inestimable. They are, of course, a rather private treasure, which is confirmed each time I invite nonfamily members to share an evening of viewing slides from past family vacations.

The point being made here is that family life, like so many of life's riches, has to be extracted and worked on. As soon as it is taken for granted, it becomes tarnished and its value is depleted. Our general culture is, at best, ambivalent with regard to the future survival of the family. We have already noted (see Chapter Two) that the minds behind the machines of production like to see potential customers as *individual* consumers so that they can move as many products as possible. If our nation has any family policy at all, it is probably oriented to the creation of laws indifferent to the real needs of the family. The Catholic Church has taken a stand in favor of family survival and enrichment. Whether the Church's plan for family ministry makes a significant impact on the vitality of family life will depend on what's done at the local level, particularly by families themselves.

What really prompts people to become involved in something they are not accustomed to doing? There seem to be two basic ingredients that must enter their motives. First, they need to have an appreciation for what they are to do as *worthwhile*. Time is a precious possession. No one willingly wastes it on what they view as worthless. They may spend their time on what others judge pointless, but for themselves, there is always something of personal value to be gained. Second, before any of us embark on a new venture, we want some confidence that we'll be successful. We'll act only if we have *hope*.

The bishops' plan also knows the importance of hope. The text of the plan concludes, in the spirit of Christian hope, with these words:

Our Christian optimism, based as it is on Christ's own victory in the face of apparent defeat, gives us reason to see a time coming when, through the renewal of the Church's ministry, a better world will come about for the entire human family.

Christian hope is based, not simply on statistical projections, but on the power of God, a promised resource released and made available through the death and resurrection of Jesus. God's promised assistance makes up half of the fundamental resource needed for the renewal of the Church through family ministry. The other half is ourselves!

The more serious and practical question about the future of families is whether the human resources will become active to their full potential. Of course, the ecclesial and social environment remains significant, but at least in theory, the ecclesial environment will be establishing a network of support and assistance. This will not, however, be enough. Something much more personal must take place if families are to deepen their life of togetherness and their commitment to ministry. In the concrete, each parish and each family must personally sense the urgency of the invitation to make family ministry a very high priority in their daily life.

To accomplish this we will have to overcome a rather fundamental law of human nature that might be stated as: wait as long as you can before you do anything! Maybe you will recognize its widespread usage if a few examples of practitioners are given. This law is followed by those who file their Federal income-tax return at 11:59 P.M. on April 15th. It is obeyed by those who enter the church one step before the priest. You'll find followers in grocery stores at closing time and in cars driving a few miles with the fuel gauge reading "E." They will also be seen driving up to airports about ten minutes before scheduled plane departures. They also send Christmas cards on December 22nd. In short, believers in this law feel that if you wait long enough, maybe someone else will do what you should be doing. One reason I know about this law is that I have followed its dictates often. So do most of the people I know.

Throughout this book, we have been discussing concepts like ministry, empowerment, responsibility and renewal. The intent was to have these words come to life around various issues that touch family life. If it has not yet become clear, let it be stated as unambiguously as possible that for its success family ministry will depend on the activization of the *laity* of the Church. Family life is an area where the laity have uncontested expertise. This is not to argue that the laity will be acting alone. The Church is a community of shared responsibility and common ministry. Given the range of family ministry, there will be ample tasks for everyone.

Each person will have personal reasons for becoming more active in family ministry. It may be out of gratitude for the joy and fulfillment already experienced in family life. It may be out of a sense that this is an area of ministry much needed in our contemporary world. It may be because the person perceives that the Christian renewal of family life is the key to effective Church renewal. It may be based on a sense that one is *called* to be active in family ministry. It may be simply, though not insignificantly, because one is a married and/or a family person.

We are also challenged by our experiences. We recall with delight special moments in our lives, and we want to live in such a way that these moments of special meaning may again be experienced. We may want those we love to have those kinds of experiences as well. Sometimes we want to live toward certain ideals. In the case of family ministry, it may be that we want to create deep experiences of Christian love and intimacy in the context of marriage and family life.

Years ago I recall hearing about a particular image of the American male that really irritated John F. Kennedy. To this day I do not really know whether the story was pure fable or not, but it does not make any difference. The effect of its telling on me remains forceful. J.F.K. was said to despise the depiction of a rather flabby, middle-aged male, wallowing in an overstuffed chair as the whole weekend passes, getting up only to change channels on the television set or to get another can of beer from the refrigerator. This image etched itself on my own psyche. Not that I knew anyone who exemplified the picture that much, but it had the power to warn me what not to become: a wasted person.

As I read it, the image is not against leisure or the value of rest and relaxation. What it decries is emptiness, laziness, apathy and idleness. The proper response is not compulsive work without rest, but a desire to be active and alive. While there may be no guarantee that the world will be a better place because of our contributions, it should at least be *different* because of what we accomplished. Of course, these accomplishments may be known only to the mind of God, but that is sufficient.

Besides sufficient motivation to become involved in family ministry, there is also reason to be hopeful that our efforts will be worthwhile. The Christian believes that the world is not simply a blank canvas on which no artist has yet put paint nor a block of fine marble into which no sculptor's chisel has cut. Rather the world is already destined to be a success story. There will be moments of failure and the worst of these will be moments of sin, but there is the power of forgiveness and, even deeper, the power of the Spirit of God released into our human history through the death and resurrection of Jesus. This has been said before, but it deserves repeating in a world abounding in philosophies of despair or indifference.

So we begin our efforts out of a belief that the world is already blessed, and that its *most* blessed inhabitants are ourselves. We are a redeemed people, but we are still struggling to bring about all that might be. To do this more directly, we engage in a process of listening to both our needs and our strengths. This is putting into practice the suggestion of Paolo Freire who developed a method of activity called "conscientization." This is a reflection process aimed at forming judgments about what is to be done based on the actual lives of people. Family ministry is not a "funnel" ministry. It doesn't pour programs into the community. Rather it seeks to draw from people the riches that are already there but undeveloped.

It is based on the conviction that family relationships are sacred. There is probably already a hesitant, yet hopeful, belief that they are religiously important. The Church must come out now and loudly proclaim that it is so! It deserves mention that God lives not only in us, but among us. While some people may have a plaque in their living room with the words "God Bless Our Home," it would be better to have said "God has blessed the people who live here." The emphasis would fall where it should, i.e., on the people.

We began this book with some quotations from one of the

few public addresses of the late Pope John Paul I. It is worth repeating some of what he said in relation to the importance of our concern, family life in the Church:

> **The holiness of the Christian family is indeed a most apt means for producing the serene renewal of the Church which the Council so eagerly desired. Through family prayer, the "ecclesia domestica" becomes an effective reality and leads to the transformation of the world.[1]**

There is "holiness" in the Christian family. There is a real presence of God. It is a sacred reality, a singular expression of the Christian community, the Church. Not only does it live for its own survival, but it is ordained to facilitate the renewal of the whole Church and even "the transformation of the world." This is not simply pious rhetoric. It is the Christian fact.

Early in his pontificate John Paul II traveled to Pueblo, Mexico, to address a most significant general assembly of the bishops of Latin America. In his homily at a Mass celebrated on the first day of the assembly, the young Pope took as his theme: "The Family: Hope of Latin America." His own words adequately detail the importance he ascribes to family ministry, as well as its decisiveness for the future of the Church. His words speak of hope and of action. The Pope feels that the Church is moving in the right direction:

> **Let me tell you how important for the family is the work the Church is doing in Latin America. For example, it is preparing couples for marriage, helping families when they experience the normal crises which, if properly understood, can be fruitful and enriching, so that each Christian family becomes a true "domestic Church" with all the rich meaning of this expression, preparing great numbers of families to evangelize others, enhancing all the values of family life, helping the**

[1]John Paul I, "On the Family" (September 21, 1978).

incomplete families and stimulating governments to promote in their countries family policy.[2]

John Paul II went on to speak of his desire to visit every family in Latin America to express both his support and his hope for their future. He asked families to be generous, if they were blessed with prosperity, with those who were oppressed by poverty. The Pope also demonstrated the value he places on family life by designating it as the topic for the next World Synod of Bishops.

The fundamental pastoral strategy rising in the Church is directed to the freeing of the Christian family for the achievement of its fullest life. It seems that so often in the past the Church was more ready to point out the shortcomings of the family. Now the word is one of support, a word expressed to draw from the family its God-given gifts. The family is being told the "good news" about itself.

Two threads are woven through the teaching about the Church in Vatican II. They are, first, that the Church is a community, and second, that the Church has a mission. Both of these qualities of Church life apply directly to the family. The Christian family is the *first* community of the Church, and from it the other levels of community life develop. The mission of living the Gospel life and sharing it with others in service is another side of family life, *essential* to its Christian meaning.

To help us understand the more important sides of life, most of us need images that symbolize in the concrete what are rather abstract ideas. As Christians we are to look upon bread as nourishment and the sharing of a common meal as community. Deepened by faith we see the Eucharist as a memorial meal of our coming to be as Christians by the death and resurrection of Jesus. Another symbol we value is that of water. Water is the source of life and in faith we believe that the pouring of water over the baptized is the giving by God of life eternal.

[2]John Paul II, "The Family: Hope of Latin America," *Origins*, 8:35 (February 15, 1979).

The flowing of water has always been meaningful to me. Across the road from where my family lives is a small stream. It is a very changeable creek. During heavy rains it becomes quite turbulent and even raging. Children are warned to keep their distance because the creek has a strange attraction for them. They want to get close to its fury. In the summer, especially if we have a dry spell, the creek dwindles to a trickle or occasionally dries up entirely.

My favorite time to be by the stream is in the early spring. It maintains a regular flow of clear and sparkling water. It is carrying off the waters that have been frozen into the land during the winter. The land is being released from the grip of the cold as it softens and relaxes to allow for the new growth of spring. Down around the edges of the stream where the leaves of last autumn remain you might notice a slip of green pushing through the soil. The earth is revealing again its power of rejuvenation. It's expected, of course, but there's nevertheless a feeling of surprise and wonder at this new trace of life.

In a sense it is always springtime in the Church. We are energized as Easter people, hopeful and accepting of what is both already present and what is coming in the New Creation. We are a people who believe that the greatest feature worth noticing on the face of the earth is the fact of life. And we believe that the gift of life deserves nourishment and support wherever it exists.

There is often a special sense of life when a family is blessed with the arrival of a new person into its midst. We have an interesting way of describing the way new persons come to be. We call it procreation. It is appreciated as the cooperative effort of two loving persons with the God of love who is the ultimate source of all life. God and humans co-create. But this is not only the pattern for the beginning of life, it is also the way in which life develops as well. We are privileged to assist God in creating life as it begins and as it grows. A most special place where life grows is in family life. And it is this life in and of the family that the Church considers most precious and worthy of our best efforts.

PATHS OF LIFE:
Family Life Program

MARRIAGE PREPARATION AND SINGLE ADULT LIVING
Leader's Manual
Popular Level Handbooks
  THE SINGLE ADULT
  YOUNG ADULT LIVING
  PREPARING FOR MARRIAGE
Filmstrips and Cassettes
  YOUNG ADULT LIVING

MARRIAGE ENRICHMENT
Leader's Manual
Popular Level Handbooks
  ENRICHING YOUR MARRIAGE
Filmstrips and Cassettes
  ENRICHING YOUR MARRIAGE

PARENTING
Leader's Manual
  PARENTING
Popular Level Handbooks
  CHRISTIAN PARENTING
  CHRISTIAN PARENTING: The Young Child
  CHRISTIAN PARENTING: The Grade School Child
  CHRISTIAN PARENTING: The Adolescent
Filmstrips and Cassettes
  PARENTING: What It Means for Us and Our Children
  DISCIPLINE IS SHOWING WE CARE
  PLAYING PREPARES CHILDREN FOR LIFE
  TEENAGERS AND SEX

FAMILY HEALING
Leader's Manual
  FAMILY HEALING
Popular Level Handbooks
  HEALING FAMILY HURTS

LIVING WITH DIVORCE
MINISTERING TO THE AGING: Every Christian's Call
Filmstrips and Cassettes
HEALING FAMILY HURTS
LIVING WITH DIVORCE

FAMILY ENRICHMENT
Popular Level Handbooks
Leader's Manual
PEACEMAKING: Family Activities for Justice and Peace
FAMILY ADVENT TABLE MATS
OUR FAMILY SCRIPTURE: Leader's Book and Family Book
ARTS AND CRAFTS FOR THE CHRISTIAN FAMILY

For more information write to:

PATHS OF LIFE
Promotion Department
Paulist Press
545 Island Road
Ramsey, N.J. 07446

201-825-7300